Text
**Mich**

# The Complete
# Loire
# à Vélo
# Trail

**BIKE GUIDE**

## from Nevers to the Atlantic

*Cartography*
**Patrick Mérienne**

Editions OUEST-FRANCE

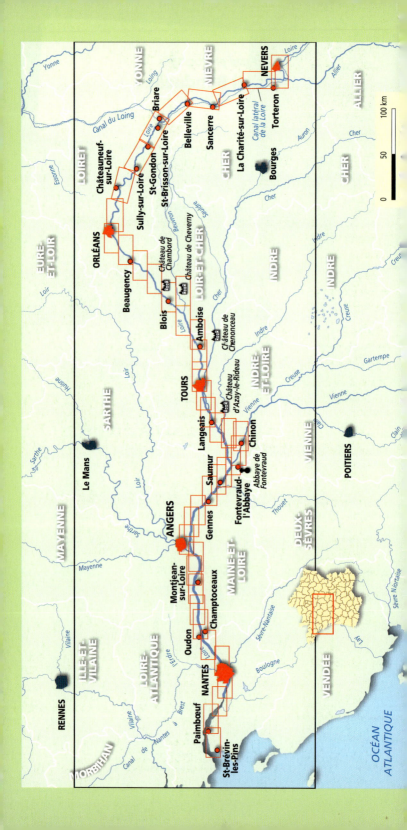

# Table of contents

*Preamble* ......... 4
*Instructions for use* ......... 6

**Stage 1**
**From Nevers to La Charité-sur-Loire**
(42 km) ......... 6

**Stage 2**
**From La Charité-sur-Loire to Sancerre**
(25 km) ......... 20

**Stage 3**
**From Sancerre to Briare**
(45 km) ......... 24

**Stage 4**
**From Briare to Sully-sur-Loire**
(32 km) ......... 30

**Stage 5**
**From Sully-sur-Loire to Orléans**
(45 km) ......... 36

**Stage 6**
**From Orléans to Beaugency**
(30 km) ......... 44

**Stage 7**
**From Beaugency to Blois**
(35 km) ......... 50

› *Excursion*
**The "Pays des Châteaux à vélo"** ......... 58

**Stage 8**
**From Blois to Amboise**
(43 km) ......... 62

**Stage 9**
**From Amboise to Tours**
(28 km) ......... 70

› *Excursion*
**Chenonceau Castle** ......... 76

**Stage 10**
**From Tours to Langeais**
(31 km) ......... 78

› *Excursion*
**Azay-le-Rideau Castle** ......... 84

**Stage 11**
**From Langeais to Chinon**
(38 km) ......... 86

**Stage 12**
**From Chinon to Saumur**
(35 km) ......... 94

› *Excursion*
**Fontevraud Abbey** ......... 102

**Stage 13**
**From Saumur to Gennes**
(19 km) ......... 104

**Stage 14**
**From Gennes to Angers**
(42 km) ......... 110

**Stage 15**
**From Angers to Montjean-sur-Loire**
(40 km) ......... 118

**Stage 16**
**From Montjean to Oudon-Champtoceaux**
(38 km) ......... 126

**Stage 17**
**From Oudon-Champtoceaux to Nantes**
(30 km) ......... 136

**Stage 18**
**From Nantes to Saint-Brévin-l'Océan**
(56 km) ......... 142

› *Excursion*
**North estuary, south estuary** ......... 152

*Useful addresses* ......... 154
*Credits and acknowledgements* ......... 166

# Preamble

The Loire is an obvious and natural guide to use if you want to discover the landscapes and inhabitants of this river. Being able to do so according to the leisurely pace of bicycle excursions along signposted and secured routes is now possible by following the green "Loire à Vélo" signs.

Ultimately, the *Loire à vélo* trail will provide 800 km of signposted and secured paths between Cuffy in Cher and Saint-Brévin-les-Pins in Loire-Atlantique for all levels of cyclists: children and adults, families and elderly people, local residents and tourists. This major sustainable tourism project by the Centre and Pays de la Loire regional councils, in partnership with the departments and towns along the Loire, offers unique opportunities to see all the treasures of the Loire Valley in a different light and at your own pace.

Along the route, signposted in both directions, cycle paths and small quiet roads allow cyclists the chance to pass as closely and as safely as possible to all the riches the Val de Loire has to offer. The fairly flat terrain, the opportunity to alter the distance of the stages and the many stopovers make the *Loire à vélo* trail a relaxing and leisurely route which is ideal for all, adults and children together.

These 800 km pass through the Val de Loire, a World Heritage Site since 30 November 2000 owing to the quality of its natural and cultural heritage: internationally famous castles, the Val de Loire's prestigious or more discreet monuments, elegant towns and villages along the riverbanks, the outstandingly varied flora and fauna… Pleasure and safety join forces on the *Loire à vélo* trail to help improve your discovery of these treasures.

Along the route, you will find places to eat and sleep in approved accomodation which reserve a personal welcome to *Loire à vélo* tourists: luggage transport, closed areas for bicycles, adapted meals, repair equipment and other services. These hotels, campsites and bed & breakfasts are located less than 5 km from the *Loire à vélo* trail. It is also possible to hire a bicycle or have a bicycle repaired by professionals who are committed to offering a dedicated service, reception and equipment, as well as facilities adapted to the specific needs of cyclists. The tourist offices, monuments and sites, also "La Loire à Vélo" certified, have all undertaken to guarantee a service suited to the needs of cyclists who choose to follow the *Loire à vélo* trail.

A change of scenery guaranteed in the heart of rich and well-preserved natural landscapes and a cultural heritage open to the world, the programme for the *Loire à vélo* trail should be followed according to the wishes and desires of each individual.

Centre Regional Council
Pays de la Loire Regional Council

For further information about the *Loire à vélo* trail: www.loire-a-velo.fr

> *Loire à vélo trail*
# Instructions for use
**Advice, handy hints, warnings**

### The very first European cycle route
The *Loire à vélo* trail is the first part of a "river cycle" route which, in France, connects the regions of Burgundy, Centre and Pays de la Loire. It is also the first section in a trans-European cycle route (Eurovelo 6: Rivers Cycle route Nantes to Budapest) which will soon become a pilgrim's route for cyclists, offering them the opportunity to follow the banks of the Loire, the Saône, the Doubs, the Rhine, and the Danube, from its source to the sea. Almost 4,000 km of greenways and cycle routes will provide soon a "soft" liaison stretching from the Black Sea (Constanza) to the Atlantic (Saint-Brévin-les-Pins).

## Loire à vélo trail / Instructions for use

### The Loire "à la carte"
This handy first "bike guidebook" has been designed to be placed in a map holder and read or consulted at any time. That is why its stage sheets have been laid out horizontally, a technique particularly well suited to the linear east to west *Loire à vélo* trail.

The same applies to the length of the stages, here all limited to distances suited to the "general public" (between 30 and 50 km maximum), as well as for the scales used on the maps. Each map has been framed to offer at least 10 kilometres of the day's stage, generally meaning a good hour-long trip before having to "turn the page"…

### As many stages as you want
Designed for families, children… and everyday cyclists, this bike guidebook aims to offer a pace and sequence of stages suited to as many people as possible: a total of 18 stages between Orléans and the Atlantic! However, the way in which they are divided up is a simple suggestion which may be adapted to your own pace, physical condition and goals. In all cases, it is always best to under-estimate your abilities rather than the opposite. The important thing is to enjoy the trip, to take time to try out its many aspects and to appreciate all its dimensions, and, above all, not to miss any of the stops or detours which will help you improve your knowledge and make new discoveries.

The key principle is that there is no point in hurrying! It is best to draw up the day's schedule according to the time at which you want - or are able - to start out (with visits to castles included). Also, define the day's programme according to what you have planned (picnic, restaurant or other) for the midday stop.

### *He who travels by bicycle takes his time*
Possible at all times of the year – except when the river is in spate – the *Loire à vélo* trail is a "journey" in its own right which may adopt a multitude of forms and formats.

Hard-liners will see it as a long river journey, which, depending on their fitness and the time they have available, may be completed in two or three weeks. However, no doubt, the majority will content themselves with enjoying one of the sections over a weekend or a short week-long break.

### *Safety above all*
There are very few Europeans (German, Scandinavian, Dutch or British) who get on their bicycle without putting on a helmet. But, many adults still cycle here without any protection, in the same way as if they got behind the wheel of their car and forgot to do up their seatbelts. For them, and for the example they give to the children they meet (or, worse still, accompany), never forget that a little click is much better than a serious accident!

### *For young and old*
Properly signposted and secured along its entire length, the *Loire à vélo* trail is accessible to all users, from 7 to 77 years of age, including the very youngest cyclists who may be transported on a bicycle seat or drawn along in a lightweight trailer (various hire companies offer these). Apart from taking care, the only difficulties you will need to take into account are the length of the stages and the duration of the trip: a day or a long weekend.

## Loire à vélo trail / Instructions for use

### *Be seen*
For a bicycle tourist, being seen and identified as such is just as important as wearing a helmet. It is advisable to wear light and colourful clothes (windcheater or fleece top) rather than neutral or dark colours. A reflective outer layer is the best guarantee of being seen immediately, especially in areas of forest, or when there is back light. Wheel fixtures, luggage or pannier reflectors and reflective bracelets or bicycle clips are also welcome. Nothing is too much when it comes to safety.

### *Gently sloping*
As with most greenways, the *Loire à vélo* trail is completely flat… well almost: less than 200 m altitude change for the 600 km journey between Nevers and the sea! A few of the detours available along the route explain the larger altitude differences.

However, here, the main enemy is the wind. The westerly wind – which used to fill the sails of the *"toue"* and the *"gabare"* boats sailing up the river - is so strong that it could even make you consider starting your journey from the sea (or Nantes) and choose to travel upstream. However, the problem with this is that, often, you will have the sun in your eyes during the first part of the day.

## Route signs

The waymarking along the *Loire à vélo* trail is faultless throughout almost its entire length. It is difficult to get lost, at least when you have all the information and maps available, the explanations in this guide, and a good pair of eyes… assisted by a good pair of glasses if necessary: the discreet - but always legible - signs for the *Loire à vélo* trail always show the right road, including right-hand and left-hand bends.

That is why this bike guidebook has not felt it necessary to provide overly precise information about the stage routes, mentioning each street, road and village, but, instead, has chosen to analyse, comment and discuss these places, above all, mentioning the route's immediate surroundings when bad weather or seasonal events force you to deviate from the route's main theme.

## The benefits of rail

The *Loire à vélo* tourist trail has one enviable advantage. Along its entire length, on the right bank, it runs parallel to a regional and even national railway line. From Nevers to Nantes, all year round, trains serve a string of local railway stations offering access or fall-back solutions for those following this major river-bicycle route. This is all the more interesting since an increasingly large number of these trains accept bicycles free of charge (information in the "Train-Vélo" brochure available at SNCF stores, from the 165 main stations in France, or on www.voyages-sncf.com, "Train + vélo" website) and a number of hire companies – "Détours de Loire" in particular, see practical pages – also offer their services right next to the main railway stations.

## Rollerblades etc.

For the moment, the *Loire à vélo* trail is only a "bicycle route". Usually, the paths available are flat and well surfaced, therefore, they are ideal for bicycles, joggers, walkers and wheelchair users: only very rarely do their technical features allow them to be used by rollerbladers.

### *Loire à vélo trail* / Instructions for use

### When to go

Although the summer season offers undeniable advantages in terms of light, the *Loire à vélo* trail is accessible all year round. Only the winter or spring spates, which often submerge the river's surrounding areas, may cut off some sections of the route and hinder a comfortable journey down this famous valley. The second half of April, although still cool, sees the river banks covered with attractive shades of green. May and June for the spring and September, October and even November for the autumn are all ideal for a trouble-free Loire journey, with availability at hotels, restaurants, campsites, self-catering accommodation, and bed & breakfast also being the most favourable.

### Climate

In terms of the weather, the mildness of the Anjou climate is not a myth and, in the summer, the sky is never dull for very long. However, the sun can be merciless so do not forget sun screens (creams and headwear), water etc. and always remember to take plenty of breaks.

In terms of temperatures and bad weather, it is always best to be prepared. In the spring, as in the autumn, gloves, fleece tops and a good windcheater are highly recommended.

## Minimum requirements for cycling

Although there are not a huge number of them, bicycle hire companies, bicycle stores and bicycle repair shops are dotted along the *Loire à vélo* trail. The equipment for hire is often of very high quality and the types of road surface are relatively harmless for bicycles, therefore it is rare to find yourself in difficulty along the route, However, in the event of having to get by on your own, do remember to take the "basic minimum": a sturdy bicycle lock, a repair kit in your saddle bag (puncture repair kit, Allen key, screwdriver, tyre-lever, spare inner tube) and, above all, a pump. Keeping your tyres filled to a maximum, as everyone will tell you, is a sure way to avoid punctures.

## Extra baggage

Except in the case of long journeys (particularly when camping), it is best to avoid carrying too much luggage. Two average-sized rear panniers with a handlebar bag or a small rucksack (which may be attached to the luggage carrier if necessary) will be quite enough for a two or three-day excursion. Keep the "front wheel" panniers for long trips (for example, *The Complete Loire à Vélo Trail*). However, never forget the all-important map-holder (for this guidebook), a small saddle bag (for the repair kit) and the bottle holder for water supplies.

## Loire à vélo trail / Instructions for use

*Castle of Ussé.*

# Preparing for your trip

- **Loire Valley Regional Tourist Board**
37, av. de Paris, 45000 Orléans
Tel: 02 38 79 95 28
Website: www.visaloire.com

- **Cher Departmental Tourist Board,**
5, rue de Séraucourt
18000 Bourges
Tel: 02 48 48 00 10
Website: www.berrylecher.com

- **Loiret Departmental Tourist Board,**
8, rue d'Escures, 45000 Orléans
Tel: 02 38 78 04 04
Website: www.tourismeloiret.com

- **Loir-et-Cher Departmental Tourist Board,**
5, rue de la Voûte-du-Château,
41005 Blois
Tel: 02 54 57 00 41
Website: www.cœur-val-de-loire.com

- **Indre-et-Loire/Touraine Departmental Tourist Board,**
30, rue de la Préfecture, BP 3217
Tel: 02 47 31 47 48
Website: www.tourism-touraine.com

- **Pays de la Loire Tourist Board**
1, place Galarne,
44200 Nantes
Tel: 02 40 48 24 20
Websites: www.enpaysdelaloire.com
and www.loire-a-velo.fr

- **Anjou Departmental Tourist Board**
(Maine-et-Loire),
place Kennedy, 49021 Angers
Tel: 02 41 23 51 51
Website: www.anjou-tourisme.com

- **Loire-Atlantique Departmental Tourist Board,**
11, rue du Château-de-l'Eraudière,
44306 Nantes Cedex 3
Tel: 02 51 72 95 30
Website: www.loire-atlantique-tourisme.com

Websites "Loire à Vélo"
www.loire-a-velo.fr
www.valdeloire.org
www.loire-chateaux.org
Websites for the 19 best places
to visit in the Val de Loire

## Stage 1
# From Nevers to La Charité-sur-Loire
## 42 km

▶ The first stretch of the *Loire à vélo* trail leaves Nevers from the south, in order to reach the north road at the junction of Allier! It is a beautiful introductory stage – natural, historical and cultural at the same time – from the capital of Nièvre to La Charité, the former passageway of the pilgrimage route to Santiago de Compostela, situated between two bodies of water, the Loire River and its Canal Latéral and between two territories, the departments of Cher (Centre region) and Nièvre… in Burgundy.

## Stage 1 / From Nevers to La Charité-sur-Loire

# Nevers in brief

Whether you are in a hurry or not, you should devote at least a few hours to Nièvre. Nevers, the town of Saint Bernadette, earthenware and "Hiroshima, mon amour" is well worth it.

Just up the road from the new SNCF railway station, the Porte du Croux, the medieval remains of the former city walls, sets the scene immediately: it opens out on to the potters' neighbourhood where, in the 16th century, the famous "Nevers blue" was developed. 200 m further on, Saint-Cyr-Sainte-Julitte Cathedral transports you even further back in time. Note its astonishing composite choir – Gothic and Romanesque – which the stained glass windows light up with glimmering colours.

The Dukes' Palace (photo left) is almost right next to the sanctuary. It is a must, especially since the Tourist Office is situated on the basement level!
The palace, the residence of the

Dukes of Nevers, but also the "second castle of the Loire" (the first titleholder being Saint-Aubin in the neighbouring department!) is considered to be one of the most beautiful built reminders of the first French Renaissance. Where is the best place to admire it from? The end of the lawn-covered Place de la République facing it, which also leads directly down to the bottom of the town and the course of the Loire River, easily reached via the Promenade des Remparts or along the steep streets which wind their way down to the Quai des Mariniers and the Pont de Loire.

*Tourist office:*
*rue Sabatier*
*Tel: 03 86 68 46 00*

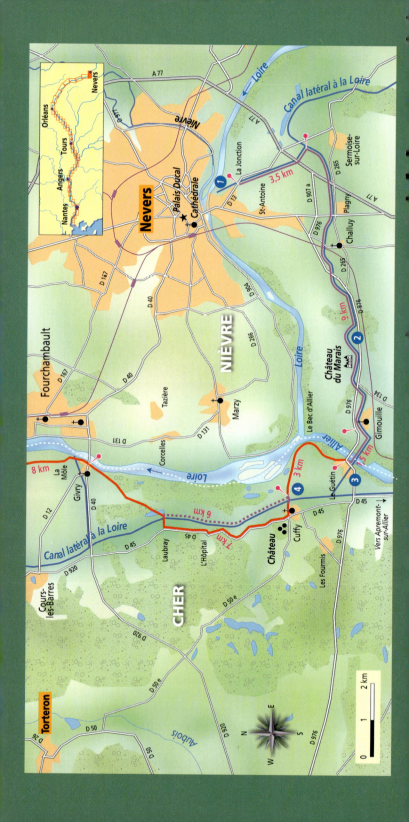

## Stage 1 / From Nevers to La Charité-sur-Loire

## A Greenway for starters

❶ Now having left the upper town, in order to reach the protected *Loire à vélo* trail, you will have to cross the Pont de Loire and ride to **the small river port of Le Port de la Jonction**. The greenway starts here and will lead you along the towpath of the Canal Latéral de la Loire **as far as Guétin** (Cher), 14 km away.

❷ Even with children, the path along the canal side is not particularly dangerous. However, you do need to be slightly more careful at the end of the route for the short passage through the village of Gimouille and the canal-bridge, which passes over the River Allier and its brand-new fish ladders. A photo stop is a must as much for the lock manoeuvres as for the superb bridge – 343 m long – over which you have just crossed the River Allier. Note that, the canal-bridge is in stone, unlike the famous Briare bridge, which you will be able to admire in the 3rd stage and which is built entirely of metal.

◆ A detour is possible to **Apremont-sur-Allier** (southwards, while awaiting the creation of a greenway). A 11 km round-trip for a delightful river setting and, on arrival, a charming village and an outstanding floral park. An incredible feat of engineering: nearby, the round lock is one of only two in France!

❸ Back to our starting point, namely **Guétin, at an altitude of 189 m**. After the canal-bridge lock, the cycle route temporarily leaves the canal and makes its way,

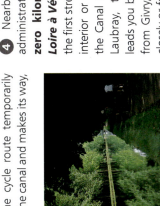

via a small traffic-free road, to Bec-d'Allier. Take a break here and enjoy the view over the confluence. In a very natural setting, the River Allier joins its waters with those of the River Loire for a shared adventure covering more than 500 km!

❹ Nearby, **Cuffy** marks – in administrative terms – **the official zero kilometre point of the *Loire à Vélo* trail**. You may cover the first stretches of the trip via the interior or along the towpath of the Canal Latéral. However, from Laubray, the signposted route leads you back to the Loire which, from Givry, you will either follow closely or from a distance.

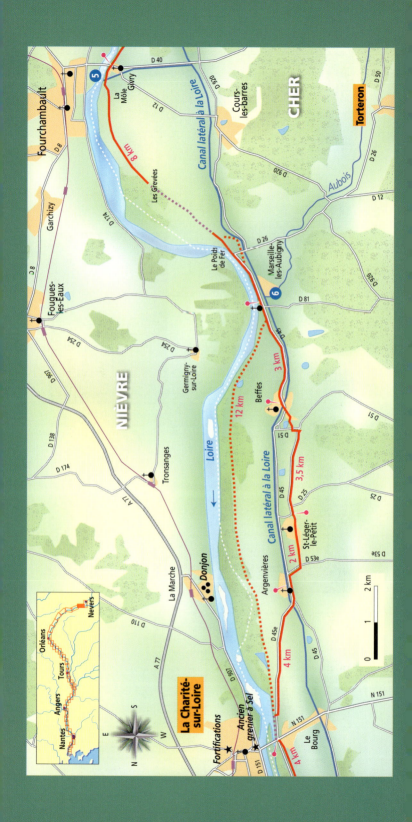

## Stage 1 / From Nevers to La Charité-sur-Loire

**5** Just after crossing the large bridge leading to Fourchambault, note the former junction canal of the Canal Latéral with its river. **Marseille-les-Aubigny**, 8 km further on, will provide you with the explanation. The huge inland waterway port was built here – at the meeting point between the Canal Latéral de la Loire and the former Berry Canal, which, via the River Cher, offered a handy short-cut to Bourges and the downstream course of this major river.

**6** After Marseille-les-Aubigny, the official route for the *Loire à vélo* trail – always well signposted – passes through about half a dozen villages and hamlets on the

*The pleasant Marseille-les-Aubigny riverside stage.*

left bank of the Canal Latéral, but, it is also possible to opt for the slightly rougher route which follows the river's "levee". The route runs alongside the river, its shady coppices, shifting islands and floodable plains as far as **La Charité-sur-Loire** and provides a beautiful introduction to the nature reserve which follows.

## Stage 2
# From La Charité-sur-Loire to Sancerre  25 km

> The short day trip will leave you time, at the end of the stage, to enjoy the many charms of Sancerre and its neighbour, Saint-Satur. Along the way, you will have the opportunity to pass through one of the best preserved Loire ecosystems: the Val de Loire reserve, with the superb and fascinating Pavillon du Milieu de Loire in Pouilly, which provides nature lovers with all the keys for understanding this unusual environment.

## Stage 2 / From La Charité-sur-Loire to Sancerre

## La Charité-sur-Loire in brief

The town is not actually on the *Loire à vélo* trail, but it would be a mistake not to go and see it from closer quarters by crossing the double bridge which leads straight to it! Along with the one in Beaugency, this bridge is one of the oldest on the Loire (16th century), and its older versions – in wood – saw the passage of tens of thousands of pilgrims heading for Santiago de Compostela after their departure from Vezelay two or three days earlier. The town's name probably comes from the generosity with which these pilgrims were received by the monks in the 11th century. Start with a visit to Notre-Dame Church (photo right), a jewel of Burgundy Romanesque art, and the maze of streets which have

helped the village to maintain its medieval character. Book lovers will be overjoyed! Now known as the book neighbourhood, the lower part of La Charité is filled with medieval-style stores devoted to ancient and modern printed works.

*En route towards Sancerre and its hill with panoramic viewpoint, you can't fail to be drawn to the gems on the right bank of the river, not least the Church of Notre-Dame!*

**Tourist office
5 place Sainte-Croix
Tel: 03 86 70 15 06
www.lacharitesurloire-tourisme.com**

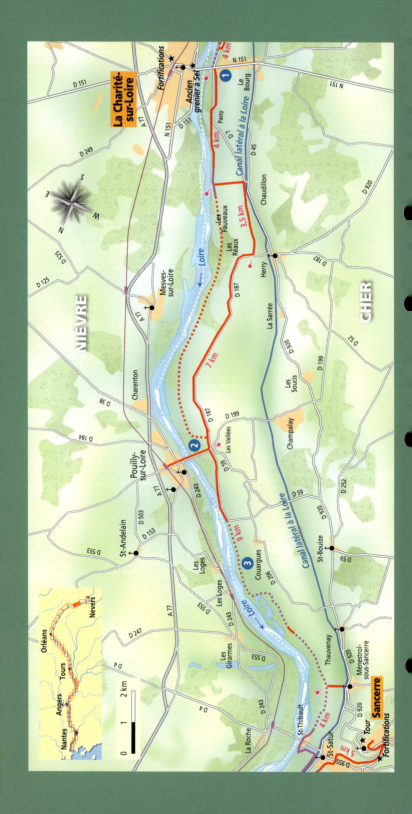

## Stage 2 / From La Charité-sur-Loire to Sancerre

**1** Back to the left bank. On the way to **Passy and Vauvrette**, as it did upstream from La Charité-sur-Loire, the cycle route follows the Loire levee. Here and there, perched precariously along it, you will see several houses, all well familiar with the river's dangers and the deceptive languor of the sand banks during the summer months. Here, the crest of the embankment passes through the huge "Loire Nature Reserve". It is time for all nature lovers to prick up their ears and open wide their eyes. With its tree-covered islands, dead channels and floodable plains, this area has become a sanctuary for wildlife.

**2** Less than 10 kilometres away, on the opposite bank, you will start to see the roofs and the bell-tower of **Pouilly-sur-Loire**, surrounded by vineyards bathed in sunlight. Cross the metal bridge over the river at Les Vallées to reach the small town and its treasures - its lively white wine, the Loire Museum and its information centre about the Loire ecosystem. Equipped with a picnic area in the same way as the previous village – but, this time, on the banks of the river – the ambitious Pavillon du Milieu de Loire has been established, very symbolically, halfway along the river's course. 496 km of water still remain before the estuary.

**3** Initially asphalted, the route along the left bank very quickly becomes a large well-surfaced track, which winds its way through the fields and tree-lined banks of the river. Although it may feel very near, the Loire is visible only very occasionally. It comes back into view on the approach to **Saint-Satur-Saint-Thibaut**, at the foot of the Colline de **Sancerre**. For cyclists wishing to ride up to the town-viewpoint, the route with the least gradient is the one which passes by here. For the others, the best option would be to follow the recommended trail to Ménétréol, and to leave your bicycles beside the Canal Latéral. It is best to climb the final section of road leading to the "roof of the world" of Sancerre by foot (312m, namely an altitude difference of 150m from the course of the Loire!). A reward awaits you at the end of the steep path in the shape of a breathtaking panoramic view over the surrounding villages, the vineyards which cover the hillsides, the Loire and its canal, and the fields where the "manufacturers" of the local "crottin" cheese graze peacefully.

## Stage 3
# From Sancerre to Briare

**45 km**

› A stage which bears witness to the difficult relationship which exists between people and the Loire River and their early attempts to tame the wild waters which, inevitably, nobody has been able to dictate.
The route starts with a long and superb section along the Canal Latéral.
It continues along the levee of the river's left bank, the imposing embankment built and consolidated century after century in order to contain the Loire's devastating spates, and ends with the technical and aesthetic masterpiece of the famous Briare canal-bridge.

## Stage 3 / From Sancerre to Briare

### Sancerre in brief

Don't hesitate to visit the Colline de Sancerre again before leaving, especially if the previous day's stage only allowed for a brief tour. With its ramparts, its narrow winding streets, the Maison de Sancerre and its wine-growing backdrop, the old town is well worth a visit! Start with the spectacular climb to the Tour des Fiefs, a 15th century keep which guarantees a 360° view over the entire area: on the one side lies Berry with Nivernais and the Loire Valley on the other... note in particular the vineyards spread out below, of which Chavignol is the most well-known, famed for the local sauvignon as much as for its "crottin" cheese!

This should be enough to give you an excuse for a picnic made from local produce. Coming back down towards the Canal Latéral via the tourist route which follows the old railway viaduct (photo right), you come straight to the neighbouring market village of Saint-Satur. The perfect time and place to stock up on food before continuing on your way?

*Sancerre tourist office*
*rue de la Croix-de-Bois*
*Tel: 02 48 54 08 21*
*Saint-Satur tourist office*
*place de la République*
*Tel: 02 48 54 01 30*

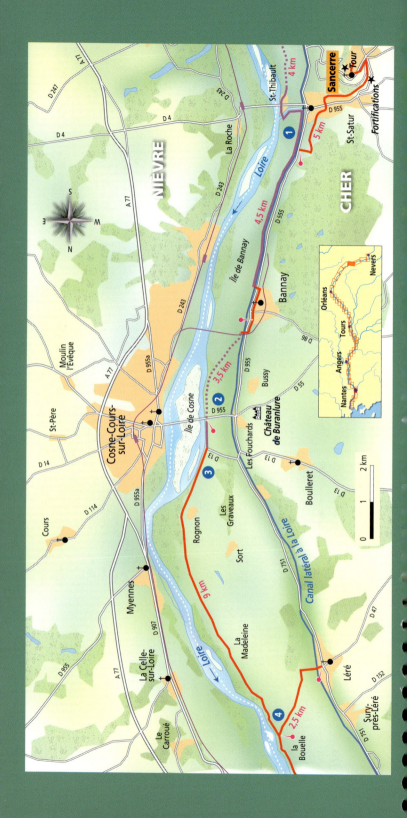

*Stage 3 / From Sancerre to Briare*

**① As you leave Sancerre**, forget about the Loire for a while! The first few kilometres of the day's stage follows the area next to the Canal Latéral. The greenway along the shady grit towpath winds its way between the peaceful Canal Latéral and the superb Sancerre golf course, before making a short detour at Bannay. After this, you will return to a route leading back to the Loire and its all-important "levee": a work realised over several centuries, the imposing size and vast movements of which are a sign of the scale of the spates which, time and again, have affected those who live alongside the river.

**②** Along the way, one detour is a must to **Cosne-sur-Loire** on the opposite bank, even if, in order to cross the double bridge, it is best to use the pavements, because, although it was built just fifty years ago, the design of this bridge does not include a cycle route! Apart from its gîtes and restaurants, Cosne offers historic remains, an inland waterways museum, an Art Deco cinema and an idyllic setting on the banks of the Loire.

**③** Back on the left bank, the route continues along the "levee" – now with a pleasant asphalt surface. This elevated position provides a view over the large cultivated fields on the western side.

**④** After **La Bouelle**, the asphalt road becomes a large, fine gravel path which, again, will change on the approach to Belleville nuclear power station, the white smoke from the cooling towers of which we will have seen from a distance.

For safety reasons, here the route is obliged to make a large bypass around the site, which includes a small detour to the border of the Cher and Loiret departments along a short section of the Canal Latéral de la Loire.

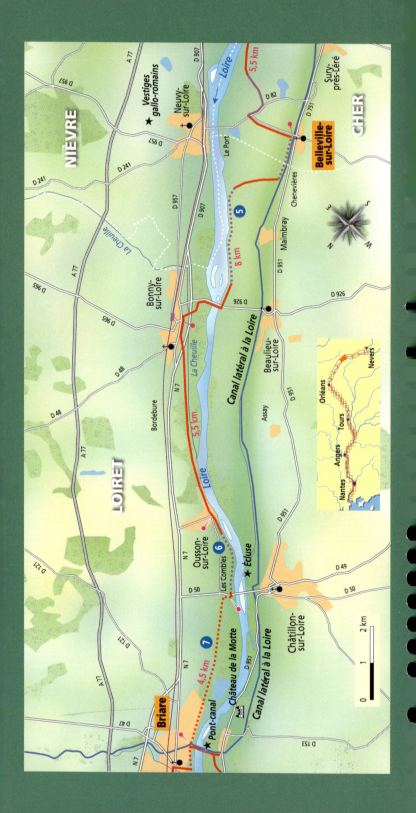

## Stage 3 / From Sancerre to Briare

**5** Then, rejoin the river bank to reach the bridge separating **Beaulieu** from **Bonny-sur-Loire**. Whether temporarily or for the duration, the official route recommends that you join the right bank here - and with reason!

Between the large town, spared by a road bypass, and the following village (Ousson-sur-Loire), for about half a dozen kilometres the cycle route passes along one of the most beautiful stretches on the "journey"! The course of a small river – **the Cheuille** – which merges slightly further on with the Loire, now more majestic and wild than ever...

**6** After Ousson, the rougher trail may spoil your pleasure slightly, but, no doubt, this is in order to prepare you for arriving in Briare. At the bridge in **Chatillon-sur-Loire**, first of all, you will see the superb, old lock of Les Combles. It used to allow Loire freight ships to make their way up a long, rectilinear reach (4.5 km which the well-surfaced route follows almost along its entire length) to the river port of Briare where, via the Loing Canal, they joined Montargis, le Gâtinais and at the end of the journey the Seine basin!

### Briare, in brief

The town of the canal-bridge (115 years old in 2011, a listed World Heritage site!) has more to boast than the logistical masterpiece which leads its canal over a Loire River as wide as the height of two Eiffel Towers! Glimmering in the radiance of its enamel work, Briare is a garden town, an attractive river port and a stopover much appreciated by *Loire à vélo* tourists, as well as by river cruisers and camper van enthusiasts.

*Tourist office:*
*1 place Charles de Gaulle*
*Tel: 02 38 31 24 51*
*www.briare-le-canal.com*

**7** A Herculean task which, today, can only be explained by the unwavering belief of its developers in the progress and promises of river transport.

## Stage 4
# From Briare to Sully-sur-Loire

**32 km**

▸ A relatively short stage, but one which will allow you all the time you need to visit the many gems along the way. First of all, Briare and its canal-bridge (a UNESCO world heritage site), then, about a dozen kilometres away, the magnificent town of Gien, and, finally, Sully-sur-Loire - its castle, its park and moats — which, on the left bank, is reached after a long and panoramic trip alongside the great river.

## Gien in brief

With its bridge with reinforced piers, the vast shores of the Loire, the castle all in stone and brick which, just behind it, masks the square bell-tower of the Church of Sainte-Jeanne-d'Arc, the town is one of the most attractive stopovers on the route along the Loire. You should spend at least a few hours visiting the first royal castle on the Loire, the Hunting Museum (for enthusiasts of this sport) and, of course, the unmissable Earthenware Museum!

*Tourist Office:*
*Place Jean-Jaurès*
*Tel: 02 38 67 25 28*

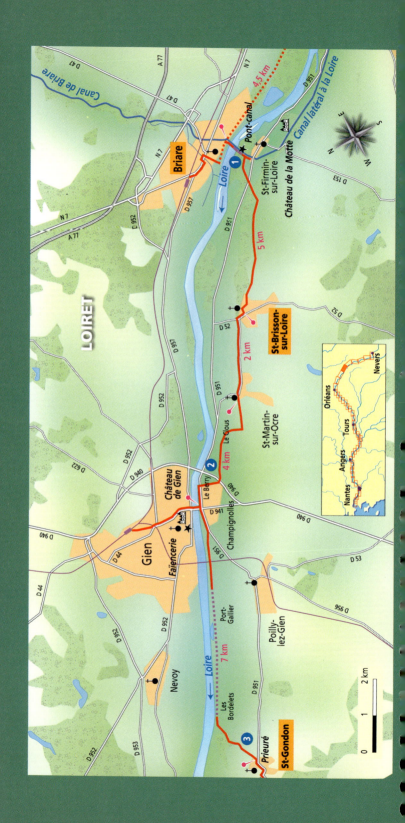

*Stage 4* / From Briare to Sully-sur-Loire

❶ Credit where credit is due, the day's route starts with a "privileged" crossing of the Loire! 600 m over the river along the downstream "pavement" of the canal-bridge which you will leave straight after in order to join the small departmental road on the left bank. The cycle route leading to **Gien** runs through a trilogy of villages named after Saints: **Saint-Fimin-sur-Loire, Saint-Brisson-sur-Loire, Saint-Martin-sur-Ocre**. Along the way, do not miss the medieval castle of Saint-Brisson! On some summer days, its fighting apparatus (catapults and others) work "for real".

*Pause for a minute to take in the panoramic view over the Loire, the bridge and Gien castle.*

❷ **Arriving in Gien** along the left bank is magical. A picnic stop awaits you offering a clear view over the Loire and the town opposite. Take advantage of this, as it's one of the most photogenic views you'll find on today's stage! All the more so as access to the town, via the imposing stone bridge, doesn't really allow for stops! There's no cycle path – or even any kind of secure means – to take you safely over the river! Fortunately, you'll soon find yourself back on the side of the castle and the Church of Sainte-Jeanne-d'Arc. An elevated square offers an extensive and pleasant view over the river.

❸ After a pleasant stretch along the river, at **Saint-Gondon**, the official route offers a long detour via Saint-Florent, but it is always possible to opt for a more direct route.

33

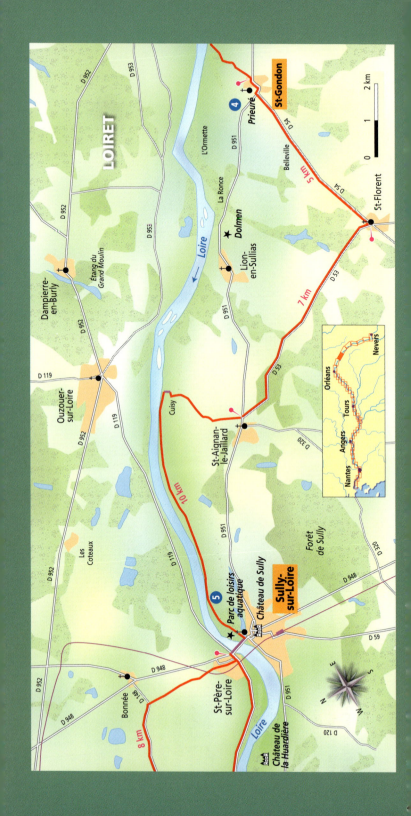

## Stage 4 / From Briare to Sully-sur-Loire

**4** Returning to the levee along a small asphalt road, leave behind Lion-en-Sullias on the left and then Saint-Aignan-le-Jaillard and head for **Cuissy**. There are still barely 8 km before **Sully-sur-Loire**, all of which follow the course of the river.

**5** You will enter the town by the castle's park and gardens; this is also the entry point into the Val de Loire which was listed as a UNESCO World Heritage site in 2000: a huge protected area of nature and culture which stretches from Sully-sur-Loire (Loiret) to Chalonnes Island on the borders of Anjou.

### Dykes and levees

Along this "upstream" section in particular, the *Loire à vélo* trail follows the long sections of the famous "levees" of the Loire, the dykes which, over the centuries, have been built and reinforced to contain the devastating spates of this great river.

An advantage of this is that these stretches are often for cyclists only (no cars, or almost none), pleasantly overlooking the surrounding countryside, the Loire, its islands and moving sandbanks, whilst offering a fascinating appreciation of the Loire ecosystem.

The disadvantage, however, is that several detours are necessary which can make the path seem rather monotonous. In addition, the cyclist is directly exposed to the strong westerly winds which prevail throughout the Loire valley. So despite the path being flat, some effort may be required!

## Stage 5
# From Sully-sur-Loire to Orléans
## 45 km

▸ A stage offering many treasures on the way to the emblematic city of Joan of Arc! Passing successively from the right bank to the left bank, firstly, the route passes Saint-Benoît-sur-Loire and its famous abbey before arriving in Châteauneuf, the town of Maurice Genevoix, along the green walkway which bears his name. The second part runs along the south bank, mainly along the "levee" which, from a distance, follows the river's wide meanders until its "royal" arrival through the park which lines the Loire southeast of Orléans.

## Sully-sur-Loire, in brief

Interest in this small town is mainly a result of its castle and the superb park which surrounds it and both will be visited with the same pleasure. The "small castle" next to the medieval fortress is the part which was redesigned at the start of the 17th century by the main minister to King Henri IV, Maximilien de Béthune, the first Duke of Sully. The keep is open to the public – and shelters the King's chamber and the oratory – so, do not miss the roof frame which carries its 600 years with pride!

*Tourist office:*
*Place du Général de Gaulle*
*Tel: 02 38 36 23 70*

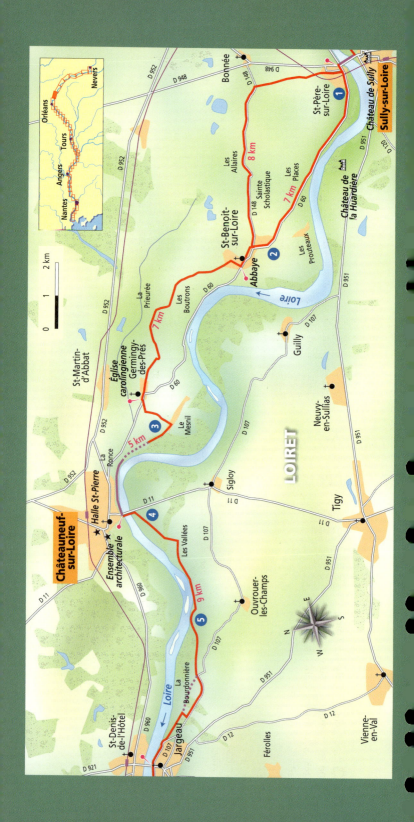

## Stage 5 / From Sully-sur-Loire to Orléans

**1** When leaving **Sully-sur-Loire**, the recommended route immediately opts for the right bank and with reason: since there are not many bridges on the river, it is the only route available if, along the way, you want to pay a visit to **Saint-Benoît-sur-Loire** and its basilica.

**2** To get there from Saint-Père, on the other side of the bridge, the most logical route is to follow the levee on the right bank. Although the islands do hide the river a little, the panoramic views over the Loire are stunning at the start and the end of the first part of the stage, especially the views over Saint-Benoît which lies in a perfect set-

*View of Chateauneuf from the Loire bridge.*

ting, far from the unwelcome traffic. From the riverside, a cycle path provides access to the large town – formerly a centre of the Christian faith – and its abbey (11th – 13th century), one of the most remarkable Romanesque buildings in France.

**3** The same thing, or very nearly, applies when arriving in the next town, **Châteauneuf-sur-Loire**. Two-thirds of the path along the levee follows a very beautiful bend in the river before a short-cut, via Le Mesnil, leads the trail into the countryside. After a small bridge, you will find yourself on a shady path which leads to the quaysides of Châteauneuf. As we said earlier, **the walkway takes the name of Maurice Genevoix** (the famous writer whose house may be seen here) and the former Loire port at the very end of it is well worth a stopover, one which is well-deserved because you are almost at the halfway point of the day's stage!

**4** The remaining part is easy: you just have to cross the bridge in Châteauneuf to join the Loire levee immediately after it on the left bank and follow it to **Orléans**.

**5** Unless there are headwinds, the trail is very comfortable and free from danger. The small road followed at the top of the embankment is asphalted all the way and motorised traffic is forbidden on certain sections

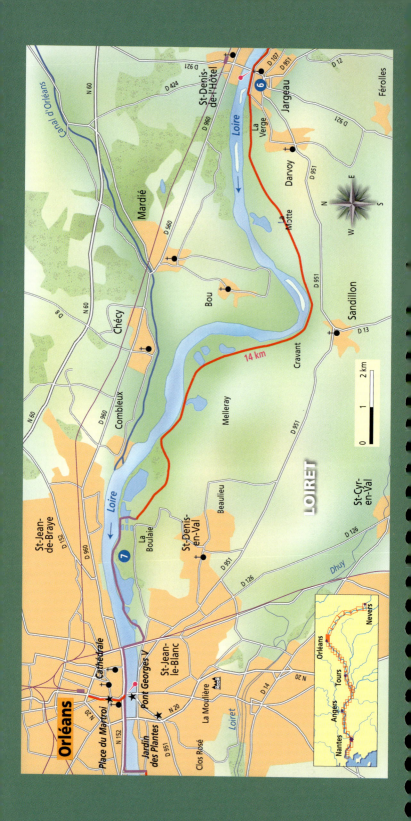

## Stage 5 / From Sully-sur-Loire to Orléans

**6** **Jargeau, the old river port,** will also provide another possible stopover on the road to Orléans, which offers an increasing number of "windows" and views over the majestic meanders of the river, its dead channels and sand banks.

*On the final stretch of the Loiret, the Loire à vélo trail hugs the great river in several places.*

**7** The arrival in **the capital of Loiret** is "the cherry on the cake" with about half a dozen kilometres of natural pathway between river and lakes which, at the entrance to the town, passes through the Charlemagne Island leisure base. A final bridge over the river, alongside the railway bridge, and you will arrive on **the new quaysides on the right bank of Orléans** which celebrate the recent reunion between the city of Joan of Arc and the Loire.

## Orléans in brief

*Sainte-Croix Cathedral.*

The city has struggled to recover from the upheavals and destruction of the Second World War, and, even more so from the town planning decisions taken fifty years ago in order to rebuild it. The city lost a large part of its historic centre in the bombing of June 1940 (17 ha, including the entire Saint-Paul neighbourhood and Rue Royale, not to mention the neighbourhood stretching from the railway station to Libération), a fact which is still visible although efforts made to recreate it have never been as great as in recent years.

This does not prevent Place du Martroi, the city's nerve centre, sacrificing itself with admirable steadfastness to the cult of Joan of Arc. Her statue, which stands at its centre, as well as, slightly lower down, Rue Jeanne-d'Arc, are immutable meeting points for celebrations honouring the Maid of Orleans every spring (from 26 April to 8 May), a national celebration since 1921, and they have never missed a single date since 1429! While you are there, pay a visit to the arcades on Rue Royale and the medieval streets of Rue Sainte-Catherine and Rue de Bourgogne. After the small Place du Châtelet, you will arrive at the Loire, on the very site of the bridge (its foundations are still visible at neap tides) which Joan of Arc seized from the English occupiers after a long and hard fight. Next to it, Pont Royal …

*Half-timber structure in the historic centre.*

## Stage 5 / From Sully-sur-Loire to Orléans

(today called George-V) only replaced it in the 18th century. Built as an extension of Rue Royale, it has since become the major historic route over the river.

Continue southwards towards the new town of La Source, with its floral park and university campus and towards the town of Olivet, on the River Loiret, which gives its name to the department. In actual fact it is a resurgence of the Loire, just ten kilometres long, which we will find a little downstream along the *Loire à vélo* trail.

*The icon, Joan of Arc, Place du Martroi.*

**Also, in Orléans, do not miss**
→ Sainte-Croix Cathedral
→ Museum of Fine Arts,
place Sainte-Croix
Tel: 02 38 79 21 55
→ House of "Joan of Arc",
3, place du Général-de-Gaulle
Tel: 02 38 52 99 89
→ Hôtel Cabu archaeology
and history museum,
square Abbé-Desnoyers
Tel: 02 38 79 25 60
and 02 38 79 20 08
→ Orléans-La-Source floral park
Tel: 02 38 49 30 00

**Tourist office:**
**2, place de l'Etape,**
**45056 Orléans**
**Tel: 02 38 24 05 05**
www.tourisme-orleans.com

*George-V bridge.*

## Stage 6
# From Orléans to Beaugency

**30 km**

▸ An archetypal halfway stage: one hour from Paris by train and situated at the crossroads of the Atlantic and the Occitan motorways. Firstly, it provides the opportunity to visit (or revisit) the city of Orléans. Also, it is an easy stage without any dangers, although the cyclist-only sections are still all too rare. It is a stage bathed in history between three towns – Orléans, Meung and Beaugency – which Joan of Arc freed from English occupation in the final weeks of spring 1429.
It is difficult not to spare a thought for her as you pass along the river banks and see the remains of the bridges seized one after the other by the Maid of Orleans during her victorious conquest.

*Stage 6* / From Orléans to Beaugency

## On the quaysides

◆ For those starting their journey at Orléans, there are **two ways to make your way through the town** from the new railway station:

◆ Either cycle through it, heading towards the river, and pay a visit on the way to **Place du Martroi** and its statue of Joan of Arc for a short, but indispensable, tour of the town before heading for the quaysides.

◆ Or, follow the recommended (and signposted) *Loire à vélo* trail. The safest and best solution.

◆ After the station, on **Place Albert I**, turn left on to the string of malls which bypass Orléans to the east.

◆ Cycle to the quaysides via **Place du 6-Juin-44**, and **Square Charles-Péguy**. Follow the cycle path along the quaysides – this time westwards – as far as the new covered market and Place de la Loire. The historic centre of Orléans lies here and may be visited on foot or by bicycle. With its tramway, car-free squares and pedestrianised streets, today, the town has intentionally opted for environmentally-friendly traffic solutions.

◆ **Coming from Sully-sur-Loire**, the *Loire à vélo* trail arrives in Orléans along the left bank. Cross René Thinat bridge to reach the quaysides and the cycle path which runs along them.

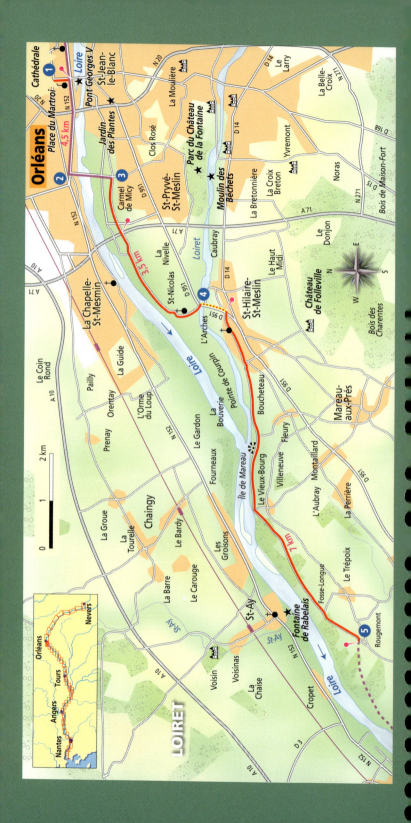

## Stage 6 / From Orléans to Beaugency

## New departure

**1** From the old Pont George-V bridge take the two-way asphalt path westwards. It is very quickly joined by a path for walkers which runs alongside the river as far as the **Pont de l'Europe**.

**2** Attractive viewpoint over the Loire when crossing the bridge (right-hand pavement), then a cycle path towards **Saint-Hilaire-Saint-Mesmin** as far as a roundabout.

**3** Turn right towards "**Pointe de Courpin**" on to a small, traffic-free and danger-free road: cars are forbidden on it slightly further on. It starts by passing beneath the A71 motorway before joining a first Loire "levee".

◆ Follow the quiet path for about 3 km to where the sign "Beaugency-Loire à vélo" leads down from the embankment to **Carmel-de-Micy**.

◆ Here, those who enjoy wild landscapes may continue to the famous **Pointe de Courpin** (a cul-de-sac). By bicycle and then on foot, it provides access to a protected ornithological reserve on a far-flung reach of the confluence of the Loiret and the Loire.

**4** Beware! Between **Carmel-de-Micy** and **Saint-Hilaire-Saint-Mesmin**, as you pass the bridge over the Loiret, the route joins the D 951. It turns on to the first street on the right as soon as it enters **Saint-Hilaire** ("Beaugency-Loire à vélo" sign), where, very quickly, you will join a new "levee".

◆ Short detour along the way via Saint-Hilaire-Saint-Mesmin Church (visible on the right) and the banks of the Loiret River.

◆ This is followed by a carefully signposted section through the countryside to Meung-sur-Loire: 11 km of "levee" and then of quiet path.

**5** Attention! About halfway along the route, leave the asphalt track for a large sandy path which brings you closer to the river. The asphalt veers towards the D 18 (Saint-Cléry-Meung) which, for those who are not paying attention, would impose the accompaniment of motorised traffic for 2 km!

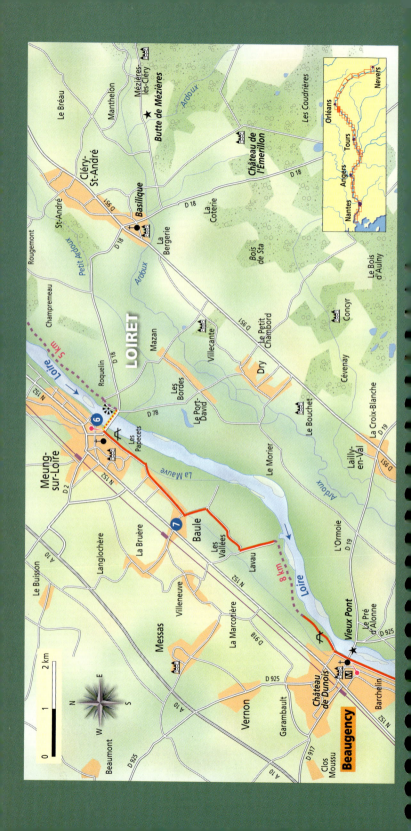

## Stage 6 / From Orléans to Beaugency

**6** Take care when crossing the **bridge in Meung**, the first bridge over the Loire since Orléans, and turn right when leaving it for this detour, 200 m on the right, to the remains of the medieval bridge which Joan of Arc seized from the English in 1429.

♦ Then, in the town centre, visit the castle (13th – 18th century), the former residence of the Bishops of Orléans, built alongside a superb collegiate church, a listed monument, dating from the 11th-12th centuries.

♦ Leave Meung by **the Chemin des Caves**, which runs parallel to a refreshing picnic area. Take advantage of a break here if you have not had lunch in the town centre. There is still 8 km left to Beaugency!

**7** You will arrive very quickly in the village of **Baule**.

♦ Take care to follow the signs to "Beaugency" in order to avoid getting lost in Mauve, an area of flood plains and orchards on the right bank!

♦ A small road, and then a large path run alongside the Loire passing another picnic stop just before the attractive town of **Beaugency**. First of all, you will catch glimpses of the arches of the huge bridge

*In Meung, the remains of the medieval bridge which Joan of Arc seized from the English.*

through the gaps between the trees: 22 arches for a total length of 440 m. A superb structure, hundreds of years old, it is the only original medieval bridge still standing on the course of the Loire.

## Stage 7
# From Beaugency to Blois

**35 km**

> A good road surface and almost entirely for cyclists only, this stage offers a rapid transition between the departments of Loiret and Loir-et-Cher. It invites cyclists to enjoy a leisurely and unlimited visit to the "Pays des Châteaux à vélo". About a dozen signposted routes and itineraries offer a wealth of historical tours and detours. First of all towards Chambord, as well as to Villesavin, Cheverny, Beauregard and a few other "gems" among the treasures of the Loire. A straight stretch of the route provides access to Blois along the right bank "levee".

## Beaugency in brief

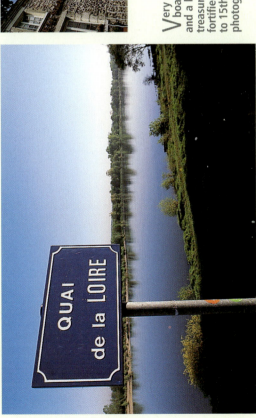

Very attractively restored, boasting small squares and a large number of historical treasures (abbey, castle, keep, fortified doors from the 11th to 15th centuries), and a very photogenic street in the lower town, Beaugency provides a perfect stopover on the *Loire à vélo* trail.

***Also, in Beaugency, do not miss***
- *Notre-Dame Church, Tour de César keep (11th century)*
- *Castle Dunois and the Orléans Regional Museum*
- *Half-timber house*
- *Beaugency bridge*

***Tourist office***
*3, place du Dr-Hyvernaud,
45190 Beaugency
Tel: 02 38 44 54 42*

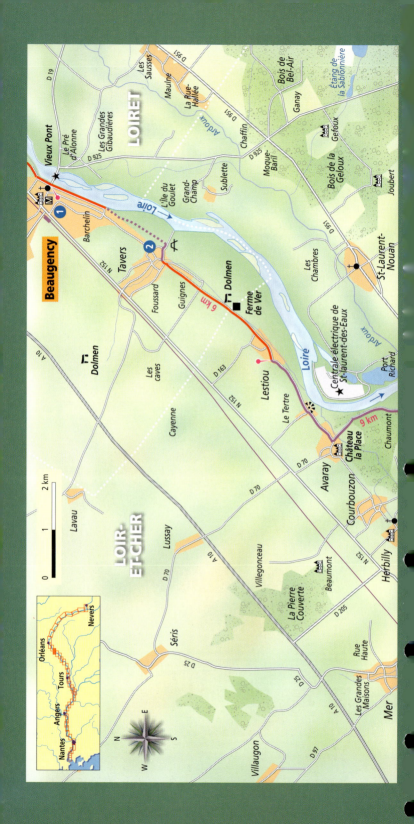

*Stage 7* / From Beaugency to Blois

## On the right track

**1** Departure point on the right bank between the old town and the Loire. The route starts with a short asphalt section followed by a large gravel section which winds its way around the river's floodable banks: this is the route of the famous GR3, the Loire long-distance hiking trail which we encounter often along the route.

**2** You may return to the asphalt path earlier. Go to the village of **Tavers,** which you will pass through along the small road leading to **Lestiou**. Along the way, do not miss the "des Fontenils" rest area, between the river and Tavers:

*Beaugency bridge, the last medieval bridge still standing on the Loire.*

next to it the crystal-clear bubbling waters are strangely muted by the moving sand beds.

◆ This is followed by an alternating series of cyclist-only sections and shared routes as far as the bridge in **Muides-sur-Loire**. A ten kilometre section bypasses the

**Saint-Laurent-des-Eaux** nuclear power station (on the other bank) and the perfect road surface is a paradise for rollerbladers.

|53

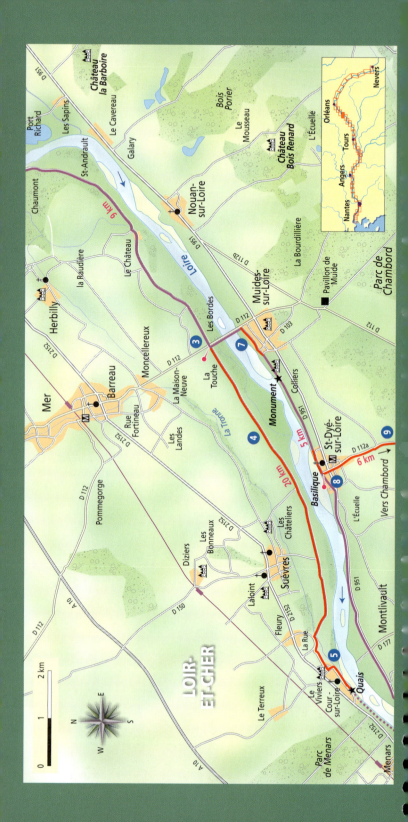

## Stage 7 / From Beaugency to Blois

③ Be careful when arriving at **Muides bridge**: crossroads with the D 112 coming from the coast, therefore, with a large amount of traffic. It is also time for you to decide: Blois or the "Pays des Châteaux"?

④ **For the quickest route to Blois**, follow the official route via the "levee" on the right (or north) bank. Undoubtedly a little monotonous, but it follows the river closely to Blois and has the advantage of not being too busy.

⑤ In the middle of **Cours-sur-Loire**, turn left towards the river to follow a path reserved for green forms of transport, then a proper greenway to **Chaussée-Saint-Victor** in the suburbs of Blois.

⑥ Continue to Southern Blois along the greenway

⑦ **For the "Pays des Châteaux"** and the approach to Blois via **Chambord forest**, cross the bridge, on foot if necessary, by the narrow pavement. Once you have done this, the signposted route avoids the traffic in the village centre and leads you along the former towpath to **Saint-Dyé-sur-Loire**.

⑧ After a 4km section alongside the river, you will arrive on the **Quai de Saint-Dyé** and the famous port which, at the start of the 16th century, was one of the most active on the Loire. It was through here that all the building material for the Chambord Castle passed! Its 900 m of quaysides are proof of this.

◆ The attraction of the "Pays des Châteaux" is irresistible. Do not miss the visitors' centre at Saint-Dyé, established in the old coaching inn: explanations, maps and itineraries are presented here. Also take a look at the brand-new "micro-garden" which has just been added to it: an initiative of the Mission Val de Loire, as part of the EuroVélo 6 programme, also visible in Joué-les-Tours, in Ballan-Miré (along the River Cher at the exit of Tours) as well as in La Chapelle-aux-Naux on the Loire, 25 km downstream from Tours.

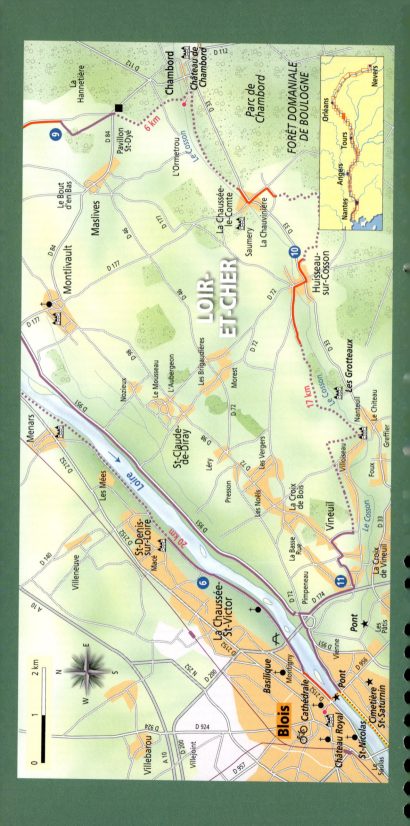

*Stage 7* / From Beaugency to Blois

## On track for Chambord

◆ Departing from Saint-Dyé, the new riverside path leads directly to Blois along the left bank. For those who, logically, choose to make a detour by Chambord, excellent waymarking has been provided and you just have to follow it from the centre of Saint-Dyé.

❾ One kilometre further on, there is a new cycle path. It starts by running alongside the road – separated from it by a hedge – and then arrives in a protected forest site which it does not leave until it reaches the castle.

◆ A road which is followed, at the entrance to the estate, by a stabilised white road surface. The first few glimpses of the castle reveal its pinnacle turret silhouette. Follow the waymarking and you will arrive very quickly at the royal site, its parking and its endless bridleways. The advantage of having a bicycle is that it is possible to ride around the park in less than an hour, including photo stops, whereas on foot it would take thrice as long.

◆ Waymarking when leaving the site is very clear. To reach **Blois**, follow "**Blois par la Chaussée-le-Comte**" a very beautiful, flat route with a white, stabilised surface, which leads to the edge of the village of La Chaussée-le-Comte.

❿ Turn left here and then right slightly further on to join a similar cyclist-only path to **Huisseau-sur-Cosson**.

Be careful not to take the D 33 between Chambord and Blois!

◆ Follow the waymarking No.1 (suggested "bis" (secondary) trail for the *Loire à vélo*). Short asphalt sections and wide agricultural tracks succeed one another until slightly after **Nanteuil**, where you will join a cyclists-only path which is large, comfortable and without any defects, although a little too short. A secure cycle path replaces it slightly further on in order, first of all, to bypass **Vineuil** and then for the final stage to **Blois**.

⓫ This final stretch does not have the same charm as the other parts of the stage. It runs about ten metres from the very "motorway-style" D 174. After the interchange before the large bridge leading to the A 10 motorway, take the cycle path towards "**Blois Sud**". However, the arrival in the "capital" of Loir-et-Cher is a form of compensation. Following the former towpath, the route offers an emblematic picture postcard view over the town, the boats on the Loire and the old stone bridge in the foreground.

## Excursion
# In the "Pays des Châteaux"
### from 16 to 32 km

> "The cherry on the cake"! A total of 300 km, 11 different itineraries, from 16 to 32 km, for a peaceful visit to the *Pays des Châteaux*, or, in other words the most sumptuous parks, gardens and residences in Loir-et-Cher (Cheverny, Chambord, Chaumont, Blois…) as well as a handful of less well-known gems, including Beauregard, Troussay, and Villesavin. An unmissable excursion for tourists following the *Loire à vélo* trail…

*Chambord*

# Excursion / In the "Pays des Châteaux"

*Villesavin*

## À la carte!

The brochure distributed by the Pays des Châteaux provides details of the 12 thematic routes on offer. These are cyclists-only paths with a stabilised reinforced surface, a sort of environmentally-friendly macadam, as well as gravel paths, often small country roads with very little traffic (about 200 km out of the total 300 km). In all cases, the itineraries are usually flat and clearly signposted, therefore, they are ideal for families. Passing through a number of villages – where you will find accommodation and restaurants – they always guarantee a peaceful journey… without the impression of being isolated which could scare off some people. The only difficulty, in view of the range of trips available is choosing between them all! To help you, remember that the itineraries most appreciated by bicycle tourists are No. 4, 5, 7 and 10.

> **The "Pays des Châteaux à vélo"**
> ➜ Brochure-map available from Bracieux town hall, 41250 Bracieux
> (Tel: 02 54 46 09 30),
> or for download at this address: www.chateauxavelo.com

*Beauregard*

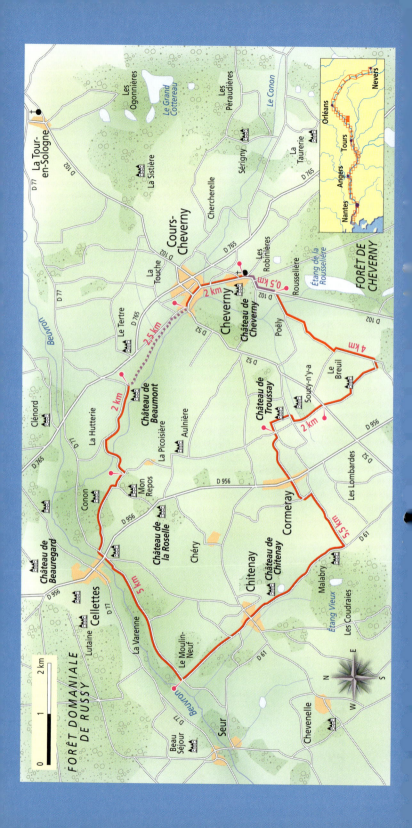

*Excursion* / In the "Pays des Châteaux"

# Key section

Chosen from the collection of 12 circuits described in "Pays des Châteaux à Vélo", circuit no. 4 can be cycled in either direction. That said, it's more logical to join it as you leave **Cour-Cheverny**.

◆ From there, there are two options – 17 or 25 km – which allow you to visit the castles of Cheverny, Troussay and Beauregard along the way - whilst alternating between cyclist-only routes and small quiet roads. The circuit is both simple and informative: passing through each village you will find a large information board explaining the history of the site and how its heritage is woven into the "Pays des Châteaux à Vélo". Virtually flat, sometimes windy (and sunny), but with flawless signposting: this route is perfect for families.

Don't miss passing through **Cellettes** (en route to the Château de Beauregard) and its superb wooden footbridge.

And on the return leg to **Cour-Cheverny**, sampling a glass of the prestigious nectar is equally unmissable! The end of the cycle path is set amongst pleasant country paths snaking between orchards and vines of the famous vintage…

## Cheverny

This masterpiece of symmetry which inspired Hergé to design his château of Moulinsart has at least two major assets. The visual perfection of a harmonious French-style garden château, and (not to be outdone) the quality of its interiors. With its original furnishings, tapestries and portraits, it's impossible, even when following the *Loire à vélo* trail, not to take time out for a thorough visit of this sumptuous work of art.

*Cheverny Castle,*
*Tel: 02 54 79 96 29*

## Stage 8
# From Blois to Amboise

**43 km**

A prodigious journey into history and heritage through the towns, sites and monuments. After Blois, Candé-sur-Beuvron, Chaumont (its castle and annual garden festival), Amboise and its attractive neighbour, Le Clos-Lucé…

A breathtaking section of the *Loire à vélo* trail, this stage has just one fault: its route often takes tourists away from the riverside. Deprived of the presence of the Loire on leaving Blois, the river only returns to view just before Chaumont! Unfortunately, the same applies to the temporary section of the route leading to Amboise, despite its being a nerve centre of Loire tourism.

## Stage 8 / From Blois to Amboise

## Blois in brief

Blois is a beautiful town which requires some puff – or leg power – from those wishing to visit it. Coming from the river and the old Pont J.-Gabriel, you will have to climb a little (or, if you want, you may leave your bicycle at the bottom) to reach the Place du Château. Dominating the town's slate roofs, it is the entry point for the castle which, since the time of François I, has made the site's reputation: a composite collection of four main buildings and four distinctive styles, from medieval architecture to the classical period, with star attractions such as the famous François I staircase and the hall where the Duke of Guise was assassinated in 1588, "greater dead than alive"!

Between the most recent Mansart wing and the recently restored chapel, do not miss a visit to the terrace: one of the rare viewpoints over the town.
A trip to the churches of Saint-Nicolas (12th-13th centuries) and Saint-Vincent-de-Paul, and the superb Saint-Louis Cathedral also allows you to visit medieval Blois. Following the paved streets, paths and stone staircases, you will arrive, at long last, at the gardens of the former bishop's palace, now the town hall. Far from the crowds of tourists, here you will be able to enjoy a panoramic view over the town, the old stone bridge and the lower neighbourhood of the left bank, through which you will depart if you follow the recommended *Loire à vélo* trail!

### Also in Blois, do not miss

➔ The Museum of Magic, place du Château – Tel: 02 54 55 26 26
➔ The Natural History Museum, rue Anne-de-Bretagne
Tel: 02 54 90 21 00

**Tourist office:**
*23, place du Château, 41000 Blois*
*Tel: 02 54 90 41 41*
*www.bloispaysdechambord.com*

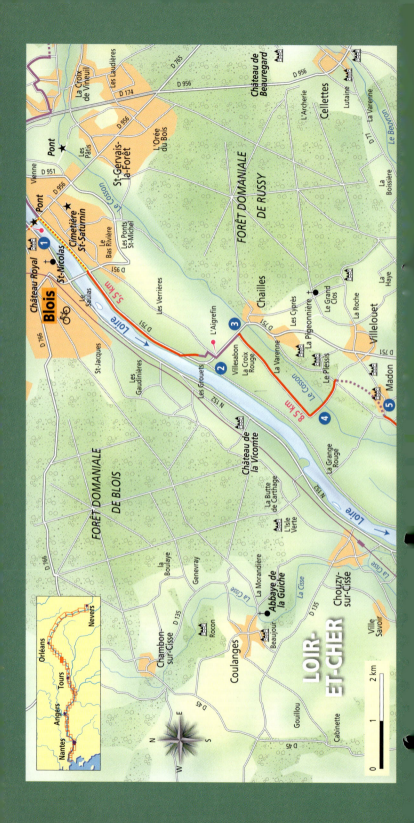

*Stage 8* / From Blois to Amboise

## Left bank all the way!

**1** To leave Blois, the only solution is to share the road with the other traffic on the left bank (follow **Quai Aristide-Briand**) at least from Pont Jacques-Gabriel (rebuilt in the 18th century after a spate destroyed the previous one) to Pont François-Mitterrand.

◆ You will have to wait until after this third bridge to join an asphalt path running below the south levee.

**2** 5 km further on, the route veers to the left along a cycle path to join a short section of the D 751 leading to **Chailles**.

**3** The path quickly joins the itinerary on the right and, again, is replaced by a new asphalt traffic-free road which passes through the fields.

**4** The road crosses the **River Cosson**, and then joins an attractive shortcut along a stabilised path just before the junction with **Villelouet**.

**5** A gentle climb up to **Madon** which you will pass through along a small road. After a short hill, the route arrives above **Candé-sur-Beuvron**.

*Blois, from the path that hugs the left bank.*

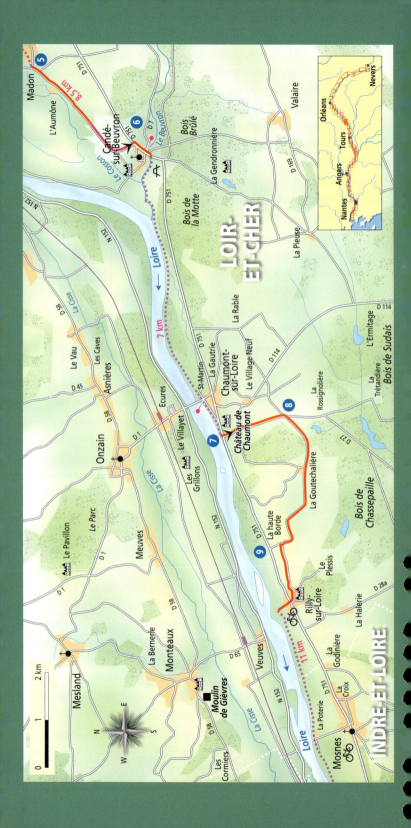

*Stage 8* / From Blois to Amboise

**6** In the village centre, turn right immediately after the old stone bridge on to the path along the Beuvron. A welcome picnic stop may be found here. The large path which runs along the waterside between Candé and Chaumont is the recommended *Loire à vélo* trail but is not recommended in the event of a river spate. In this case, you will have to take a comfortable detour via the D 751!

However, the path running along the Beuvron for 7 km allows you to get back in touch with the river which has been out of sight since leaving Blois.

**7** When arriving in **Chaumont**, the path passes the campsite superbly located on the banks of the river, before passing below the modern bridge between **Chaumont** and **Onzain**.

◆ If you want to climb up to the castle, its panoramic viewpoint and the fabulous gardens straightaway, turn left as soon as possible. Otherwise, the grassy banks of the river on the right provide a generous green carpet for a break.

◆ On the way from Amboise to Chaumont, the *Loire à vélo* trail offers very few opportunities to follow the riverside. Therefore, we recommend a danger-free secondary route... which does have a few hills!

## Chaumont-sur-Loire in brief

Chaumont Castle is well worth the effort required to climb the outcrop on which it is perched. Purchased by the Centre region in 2006, this jewel of the Loire offers a host of assets including its view over the river, its architecture and the sumptuous apartments and gardens which surround it. Every year, the ephemeral gardens attract hundreds of thousands of visitors for the famous Garden Festival.

**Tel: 02 54 20 99 22**

**8** Immediately after leaving the castle, do not miss the junction on the D27 (towards **Vallières-les-Grandes**) and turn right to **La Goutechalière**.

**9** The route then winds its way through fields, vineyards and small woods and crosses the D751 before arriving at **Rilly-sur-Loire**.

|67

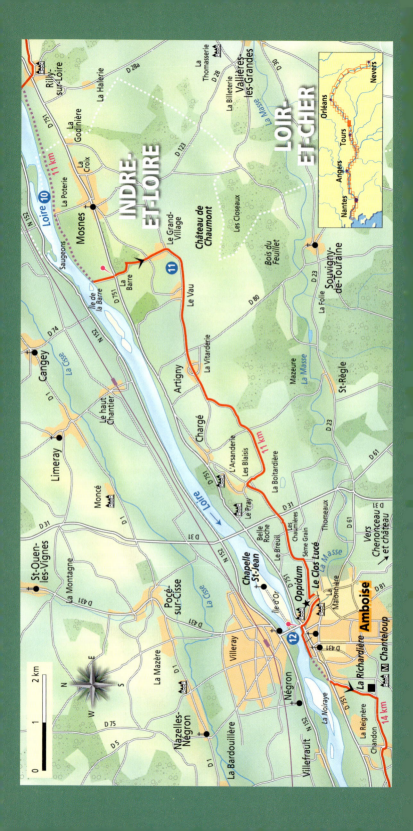

## Stage 8 / From Blois to Amboise

◆ At the crossroads in **Rilly-sur-Loire**, retrace your route a few dozen metres on the right and turn left on to a small road towards the river bank. Follow a rustic, but pleasant, and shady path and turn left towards the hamlet.

**10 Be careful!** Do not turn right too quickly towards Mosnes, the signposting may be confusing.

**11** While waiting for the Indre-et-Loire department to extend this path along the riverside, you will have to settle for a climb up to the plateau along the small road leading to **Grand-Village**, then turn right and follow the contours of the land towards **Artigny** and **Chargé**. Almost completely deserted, but exposed to the wind and the sun, so take care…

**12** Arriving in **Amboise** above the town, the route passes an orientation table before heading down to **Clos-Lucé**. Pay a visit to Leonardo da Vinci and his works (see inset on the next page) straightaway… or delay the visit until the following morning: the country seat of the ingenious Leonardo is just a few hundred metres from the town centre, less if you have decided to follow the detour to the south towards Chenonceau (25 km round-trip), and freewheel down to the town centre and the entrance to the castle.

*The Loire at Chaumont.*

## Stage 9
# From Amboise to Tours

**28 km**

› This short section of the *Loire à vélo* trail has the advantage of giving you plenty of time. For example, by allowing you to revisit a few "monuments" in Amboise before getting on your bicycle: they are well worth it, whether the castle overlooking the town, or Clos-Lucé which presents the genius of Leonardo da Vinci, within easy cycling distance of the castle… And, also, to leave time – especially for good cyclists – to make the large detour south via Chenonceau. But, be careful, if you do this, the stage will cover about fifty kilometres along non-secure roads, many of which are very busy, especially in the summer.

*Stage 9* / From Amboise to Tours

## Amboise in brief

The town is the main logistics platform for the most prestigious castles on the Loire with almost all of them located within 100 km of it! There are many Americans here, certain of seeing the very best of what is on offer, something they are always fond of. In all cases, Amboise Castle and the famous

Clos-Lucé (photo left) will keep you busy for a whole day, or, at least, two half-days. The castle is interesting, first of all, for its two powerful towers: the Tour des Minimes which is accessed by a long ramp barely accessible on horseback, which offers a view over the town which is one of the most beautiful views in the Val de Loire and the Tour Hurtault, which you reach after visiting the Logis-du-Roi, the Louis XII-François I wing and the gardens surrounding the castle to the east. Barely a few minutes away on foot or by bicycle (an underground passage way is said to join the Clos to the castle), do not miss the tribute to Leonardo da Vinci, who spent the final four years of his life here sketching a wealth of plans and preliminary projects, each more ingenious and visionary than the next. Some of them are shown here in models or life-size displays inside the manor house as well as around the Italian-style park which surrounds it. For campers, note the facilities offered by "l'Ile d'Or", the island opposite the castle. In addition to peace and quiet, the site offers an incomparable picture-postcard view over the Loire and the town of Amboise.

*Tourist office:*
*Quai Général-de-Gaulle,*
*37400 Amboise*
*Tel: 02 47 57 09 28*
*www.amboise-valdeloire.com*

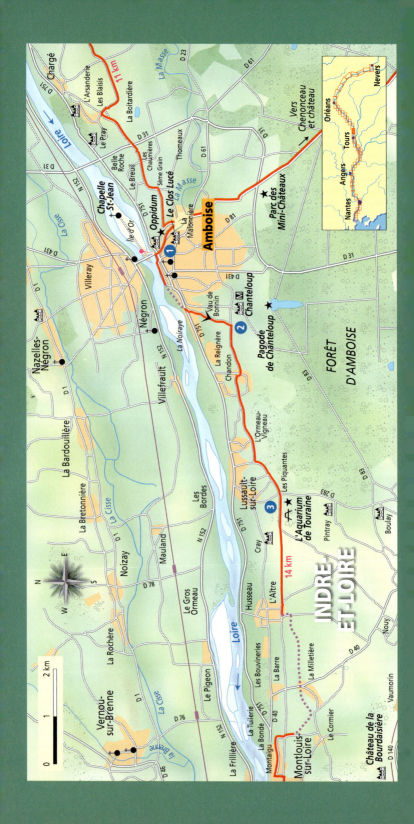

# Stage 9 / From Amboise to Tours

## Along the GR 3

**❶** The road out of Amboise is still slightly dangerous, so be careful after turning on to the left bank quayside towards Tours (and passing the Tourist Office): turn left as you leave the Noiraye neighbourhood on to the street leading to **Rue du Vau-de-Bonnin**.

**❷** Follow the small road along the hillside and continue to **Montlouis-sur-Loire**. This almost completely straight road is the path for the GR 3, the famous Loire hiking trail with its highly visible waymarking. The quiet and relatively flat route runs through fields, pastures and vineyards. The only inconvenience is that its location exposed to the elements: wind, rain, or sun depending on the seasons.

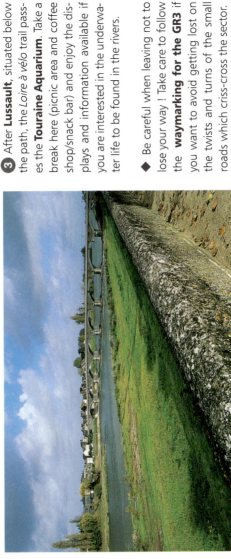

*Banks of the Loire in Amboise.*

**❸** After **Lussault**, situated below the path, the *Loire à vélo* trail passes the **Touraine Aquarium**. Take a break here (picnic area and coffee shop/snack bar) and enjoy the displays and information available if you are interested in the underwater life to be found in the rivers.

◆ Be careful when leaving not to lose your way ! Take care to follow the **waymarking for the GR3** if you want to avoid getting lost on the twists and turns of the small roads which criss-cross the sector.

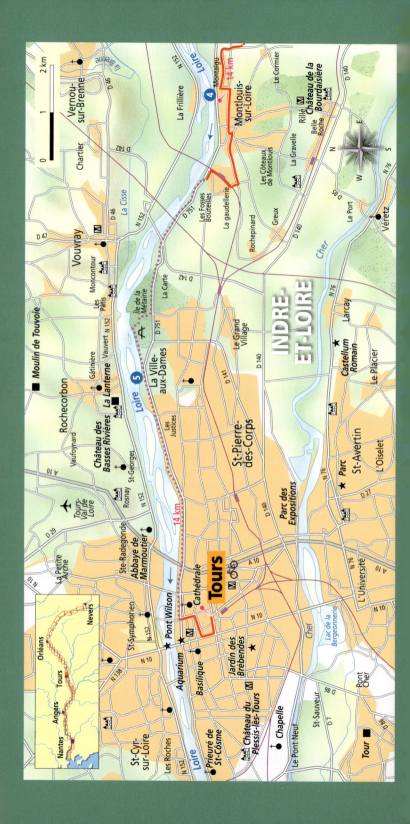

## Stage 9 / From Amboise to Tours

*A promise kept! Upstream from the town, Tours now offers bicycle access which is just as comfortable as its "downstream" exit.*

**4 Montlouis** awaits you at the bottom of the final freewheel descent and you will cross the town through its centre. When leaving the town, veer towards the Loire in order to avoid the traffic on the D 751 for as long as possible...

◆ The Montlouis-Tours stretch of the *Loire à vélo* trail is well-surfaced and follows the only path available which allows you to escape from the cars on this section. Dipping down from the road, after the TGV high-speed rail bridge, it runs alongside **Métairie Island** (the former Rochecorbon Island), a nature reserve listed by the Indre-et-Loire Departmental Council and a haven of peace. For a few kilometres, the path is good, wide and equipped with benches and picnic facilities.

**5** To reach the centre of Tours, the path passes below two busy bridges in a relatively unattractive environment, but it does run close to the river.

◆ At least, in the **centre of Tours**, you will find a better environment well adapted to bicycles. With a large number of cycle paths and, more often than not, priority given to cyclists, the town is a model which shows the way forward. This model has already been followed in the downstream section between Tours and Vilandry and bicycle tourists will be delighted to discover it the following morning.

75

## Excursion
# Chenonceau

**25 km**

▸ Difficult to pass so near (about a dozen kilometres from the *Loire à vélo* trail) without paying a visit to one of the most beautiful and most prestigious castles in the Valley of the Kings! Those willing will just have to overcome the difficulties of the temporary route available from Amboise: the "secured" route to Chenonceau Castle will not be completed for several years… Fortunately, a signposted route (see outline on the map on page 72) endeavours to avoid heavy traffic (further information from the Tourist Office).

## Excursion / Chenonceau

### Chenonceau in brief

With its flood-lit arches spanning the Cher, the magnificent gardens and the surrounding green riverbanks, Chenonceau Castle is one of the jewels of the Val de Loire. Unusual (it is built on the water), phantasmagorical (it was the home of Diane de Poitiers and Catherine de Medici), it is rightfully one of the most visited in France. Its 800,000 yearly visitors make it the second castle in France! The main stars of the site are the chambers of François I and Louis XIII, those of Diane de Poitiers and Catherine de Medici, of course. But, also, and above all, the long gallery which joins the two banks of the Cher. Out of interest, between 1940 and 1942, it was one of the "secret" passages on the demarcation line providing access to the south zone. Do not miss the sumptuous French-style gardens laid out on both sides of the central alley.

*Château de Chenonceau,*
*Tel: 02 47 23 90 07*

*Tourist office:*
*1, rue Bretonneau,*
*37150Chenonceaux*
*Tel: 02 47 23 94 45*

### Departing from Amboise

◆ At the foot of **Amboise Castle**, start by going to Clos-Lucé and then follow signs to the **Parc des Mini-châteaux** (see page on page 46). Be careful, because the D 81 is very busy and also has many bends and upward and downward hills!

◆ Turn right at the **crossroads of Grande Allée des Jumeaux** and follow a network of small and relatively quiet roads for about 5 km through a pleasant forest setting. Pass through **Mesvres** and **Chevrolière** to reach the village of **Civray-de-Touraine**… and the D 40 to **Chenonceau**. The masterpiece is not far off now.

◆ For the return road after your visit? There are two possible solutions: either return to Amboise along the same path as on the way there. Or – easier, safer and more comfortable – take your bicycle with you on the next TER train to Tours. The station is right next to the castle! Before you know it you will be back in the capital of Tourangelle.

## Stage 10
# From Tours to Langeais

**31 km**

▲ This very natural and restful stage has become a must on the *Loire à vélo* trail and rightfully so. It combines all the landscape, historical and logistical assets you could dream of finding in Val de Loire.

From the banks of the River Cher to the river port of Savonnières, via Villandry and its stunning gardens… you will then follow a very quiet section of the left bank "levee" to reach the bridge leading to Langeais.

The very bravest – or fittest – may decide, slightly before, to enjoy a twenty-kilometre detour to Azay-le-Rideau and the banks of the River Indre.

## Stage 10 / From Tours to Langeais

## Tours in brief

The "capital" of Indre-et-Loire is, along with Orléans and Nantes, one of the three major towns in the Loire Valley. A town crossed by a motorway, but, in the same way as Orléans, subject to the constraints of two SNCF railway stations (the town centre terminus and the Saint-Pierre-des-Corps "nerve centre"): for departures as for arrivals, you will often have to pass both stations! Fortunately, the town has a large pedestrianised centre with a wide choice of cycle paths and facilities for soft traffic. Do not miss a visit to Saint-Gatien Cathedral, a major heritage site in the town, which presents three hundred years of Gothic architecture, from the 13th to the 16th century.

Also, pay a visit to Pont Wilson, the symbol of the town's determination to maintain a durable passageway between the two Tourangelle shores. In its two hundred and fifty year lifespan, almost all of its 15 arches have been undermined by a combination of river spates and bombing.

Also in Tours, do not miss
→ Museum of Fine Arts, 18, place François-Sicard – Tel: 02 47 05 68 73. In the former archbishop's palace (17th -18th century), a beautiful anthology of European painting from the 15th to the 19th century.
→ Tours Castle. All that remains are two towers which are home to the Historial de Touraine and a tropical aquarium.

→ Vinci Congress Centre. Directly opposite the main station, the work of Jean Nouvel, one of the rare – and very successful – attempts at modern art in the town.
→ Compagnonnage Museum. 8, rue Nationale (near Pont Wilson). History and account of a "Tour de France" which is unique in the world. An invitation to mobility, the compagnonnage apprenticeship was designed to encourage its members to "travel around France" and to enrich their knowledge and skills. Since they were on foot, they did not have any other choice! No doubt, they would have followed the Loire à vélo if they could have...

**Tourist office:**
**78-82, rue Bernard-Palissy**
**Tel: 02 47 70 37 37** (opposite the station, to the right of the Congress Centre)
**www.ligeris.com**

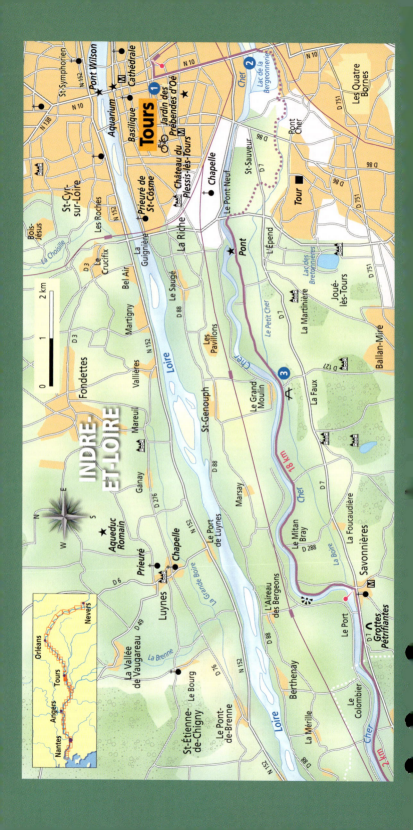

## Etape 10 / De Tours à Langeais

◆ A key section on the *Loire à vélo* trail, the stage from Tours to Langeais is an ideal excursion for families. From the centre of Tours to the confluence of the Cher, the first twenty kilometres follows an authentic greenway which is protected along its entire length as far as Villandry Castle and gardens. A flat and easy route along the Cher, better suited to bicycles than to rollerblades.

**1** From **Tours railway station**, the long cycle path on **Avenue de Grammont** (N 101) has the inconveniences of an urban path and follows the service road as far as the bridge over the Cher and its neighbouring lake, the **Bergeonnerie**.

*Along the beautiful Loire à vélo trail, on the banks of Savonnières.*

**2** This is the true starting point of the greenway. The path starts by running along the south shore of the lake, the **Deux-Lions** university neighbourhood and **Gloriette park** (120 ha) before arriving on the banks of the River Cher. From there, you will find yourself in a natural setting as far as Langeais, Chinon and Candes-Saint-Martin…

**3** A first purpose-built stopover offers the opportunity to take a break at the **Grand-Moulin**, a mill built on the course of the Cher in the 16th century, although nothing prevents you from continuing to **Savonnières** without stopping. The path (reinforced stabilised) encourages you to do so and the former river port is well worth a visit! Take time to enjoy the site and to admire the authentic Loire boats moored here. Toues, gabares and futreaux all offer summer excursions along the Cher on traditional Loire river boats!

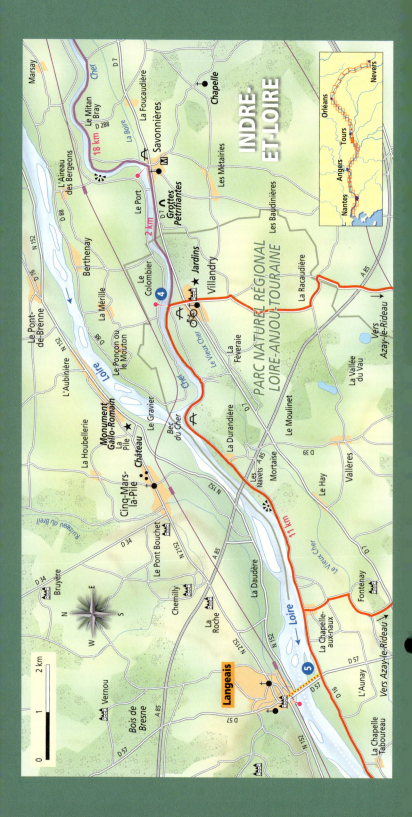

## Etape 10 / De Tours à Langeais

④ 3 km further on, Villandry, an incomparable castle and French-style gardens, appears on the left. Do not miss the breathtaking view from the terrace-keep over the geometric flowerbeds, the water features and the vegetable plots.

◆ From Villandry to Ussé (next stage), a 25 km road along the "levee" awaits you initially to Langeais and then to the confluence of the Indre and the great river.

◆ A shared road, but, fortunately, one which is not very busy, allows you to discover a superb stretch of the Loire dotted with untamed islands and historic castles, including Langeais, the silhouette of which appears very soon encouraging you to make an "excursion" to the right bank. A must!

⑤ Be careful when crossing the Loire, the pavement on the bridge is too narrow for a pedestrian pushing a bicycle. Therefore, to reach Langeais, you will have to share the road with the traffic over the suspension bridge with neo-Gothic towers.

## Villandry marquetry

Impossible to pass by this jewel of the Loire without stopping. In 2006, it celebrated "its one hundred years of embellishment". The Carvallo family, the owner of the site since 1906 has continued to repair and rebuild the Renaissance castle's roofs and facades and to reinterpret the layout, style and diversity of the parks and flowerbeds which surround it. All of this has produced a breathtaking result: barely a few hundred metres from the greenway, the castle, its parks and water features cover 7 ha which, even at the height of summer, offer a haven of peace, a delight to the eyes and a place for contemplation, particularly appreciated by those who have just cycled 21 km. A restaurant at the entrance to the castle, a few inns in the town centre and a shady picnic area next to the Tourist Office all add to the pleasure of the outing.

*Villandry Castle,*
*Tel: 02 47 50 02 09*
*Website: www.chateauvillandry.com*

## Excursion
# The Castle of Azay-le-Rideau

**16 km**

› After visiting the right bank, the town of Langeais and its castle, Azay-le-Rideau awaits you. From Langeais, return to the left bank of the levee and retrace your steps slightly – to avoid taking the D 57 – in order to reach Azay-le-Rideau along an almost entirely traffic-free route.

*Escapade* / Le château d'Azay-le-Rideau

## Shortcuts

◆ From **Chapelle-aux-Naux**, a series of small, quiet roads offer you the choice of passing either through **Fontenay** and **La Bobinière**, or through **Perrée-Groslot** and **Lionnière**. Winding through pastures and orchards, of which there are many in the area, the route climbs slightly along the way, but, your reward for this lies at the end, less than 8 km from the river: **Azay-le-Rideau**, the liveliness of its paved streets, the discreet charm of its castle, not to mention the refreshing park which surrounds it.

◆ Alternative solution: from Villandry, take the new "branch" created by the Touraine Department in summer 2007. The only inconvenience is that it deprives you of the show offered by the first part of the Loire levee which leads to Langeais. However, the advantage is that it allows you to travel to Azay directly along a peaceful forest trail through the Loire-Anjou-Touraine regional nature park.

◆ When you arrive in **Villandry**, follow the signposted route to **Azay-le-Rideau**. It runs along communal roads and a section of the D39 which, fortunately, is not very busy.

## Azay-le-Rideau in brief

An attractive small town, or rather a neighbourhood if you limit yourself to the area around the castle, a Renaissance masterpiece built on an island on the River Indre. In the 16th century, the Castle of Azay-le-Rideau was built to replace an ancient stronghold built there in the Middle Ages. Its Italian-style charm is well suited to the principle of defensive architecture: machicolations, towers, moats, battlements. The visit is a delight (access by bicycle is possible as far as the entrance) and should be completed by a visit to the surrounding park. There are so many trees that the castle is hidden from view. Those who are brave enough – or strong enough – to make the detour from the Loire will not regret it.

And will they have enough energy to continue to Saché, village and retreat of Balzac before being the home of the sculptor Alexandre Calder? The great author's museum is just 6 km away and the beautiful village of Saché is well worth the detour. However, to get there, you will have to share the D 84 with the traffic.

*Castle of Azay-le-Rideau,*
*Tel: 02 47 45 42 04*
*Castle of Saché,*
*Balzac House-Museum,*
*Home of Balzac*
*rue du Château, 37190 Saché*
*Tel: 02 47 26 86 50*
*Tourist office:*
*4, rue du Château*
*Tel: 02 47 45 44 40*
*Website:*
*www.ot-paysazaylerideau.com*

## Stage 11
# From Langeais to Chinon

**38 km**

▸ First of all offering one of the most beautiful sections of untamed Loire, this second part of this stage joins the River Vienne beneath the ruined walls of Chinon Castle. Before this, Bréhémont and the south levee of the Loire will have delighted "landscape artists", the Castle of Ussé will have enchanted those who enjoy fantasy and the confluence of the Indre will be a joy to ecotourists.

*Stage 11* / From Langeais to Chinon

## Langeais in brief

The main curiosity in the town is undoubtedly the bridge over which you arrive on the *Loire à vélo* trail route, therefore from the south bank of the river.

Rebuilt in 1950 for the fourth time in its history, this astonishing old-style suspension bridge is, apart from the motorway, the only bridge over the river between Tours and Bourgueil (45 km)! The second curiosity is the castle, which was commissioned by Louis XI in the middle of the 15th century to protect this part of the Loire from a feared incursion by the Duke of Brittany. This explains its resolutely fortified appearance compensated for by a much more human interior. It was here that in 1491, Charles VIII married Anne of Brittany. Two high-level passageways should be visited: the covered way which runs around the fortress's facade providing a beautiful viewpoint over the town and the river; and the keep, the oldest of its kind in France. Ten centuries old and still all its own crenulations!

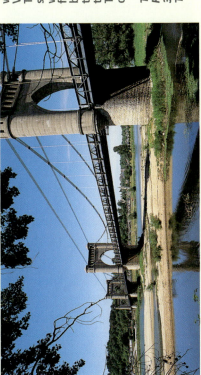

*Tourist office:*
*Place du 14-Juillet,*
*37130 Langeais*
*Tel: 02 47 96 58 22*

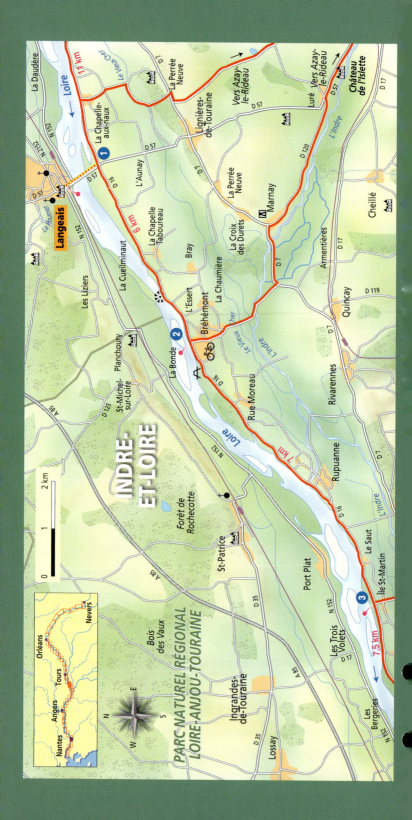

## Stage 11 / From Langeais to Chinon

## Along the river

**1** In order to return to the *Loire à vélo* trail from Langeais, cross the Loire over the old suspension bridge and follow a short section of the road to the crossroads with the left bank levee. Continue along the same pleasant path by the riverside, which you have followed since Villandry and the confluence of the River Cher, towards **Bréhémont**.

◆ From **Azay-le-Rideau** (if you have opted for this attractive detour upstream from Langeais), the route is just as easy. Take the D 120 to the levee on the south bank of the river.

◆ Via **Marnay**, first of all, and its Maurice-Dufresne Museum: varied collection of hundreds of old machines ranging from an aeroplane by Blériot to General de Gaulle's Buick, including tractors, carriages and breakdown trucks from a different age!

◆ The two successive shortcuts from the River Indre lead to the delightful Loire port of **Bréhémont**… and mark a return to the *Loire à vélo* trail.

**2** Overlooking the river, the levee at Bréhémont offers a magnificent view over the Loire which is enhanced by the paved quaysides and the old-style boats (toues, gabares and futreaux moored on the water). This is followed by a few perfect kilometres along an asphalt path, which, although in theory, is not very busy, still requires a great deal of attention from cyclists in view of the presence of motorised traffic.

*The river port in Bréhémont.*

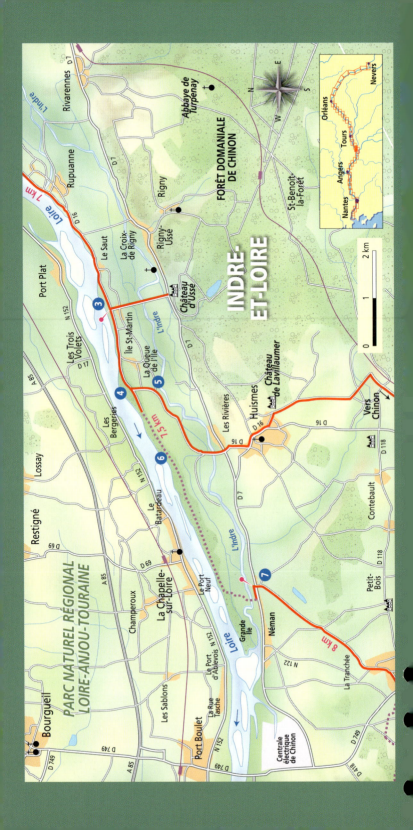

## Stage 11 / From Langeais to Chinon

**3** Fascinated by the landscape, it is easy to miss the turn! **Be careful,** you will need to turn left at the earlier Rigny-Ussé sign – to enjoy the view over "the Castle of Sleeping Beauty". A 3 to 4 km round-trip, but one which you will regret leaving out!

**4** After visiting Ussé, follow the same path to the levee and continue along the cycle path on the left bank of the Loire. **Be careful!** Slightly further on, the road leaves the embankment heading for **Huismes** whereas the cycle path continues along the same route.

**Note the new signposted route! 5** First option for reaching Chinon: just after La **Hudaudrie**, this signposted (and shared) stretch of road offers the opportunity to travel to Chinon directly (about twelve kilometres) without going as far as the confluence with the River Indre. It is an interesting option – you will save time – with an attractive landscape, but it is also much more physical with a number of steep hills on the way to Chinon.

**6** The traditional *Loire à vélo* trail continues straight ahead along a wide path which is slightly stony but carefully reshaped after each river spate - about 5 km of path with good shade and protection from the wind provided by large trees. This is what is known as an alluvium forest and it is a listed natural area.

> ## Ussé, Sleeping Beauty's castle
>
> Authentic and feared fortified castle built in the 15th century, Ussé changed considerably over the following three centuries to become a fantasy fairytale palace not too far removed from the enchanted world of Disney productions. The gently sloping French-style gardens, the romantic arbours, the terraces, the sculpted windows and dormers and the orangery all create a dreamlike site which is almost unique in the Loire valley. It is impossible to pass within reach of its towers without falling under its spell!
>
> *Castle of Rigny-Ussé,*
> *Tel: 02 47 95 54 05*

**7** The path leads to the **confluence of the Indre** and the Loire. A small bridge just before it crosses the River Indre for the last time to reach the small hamlet of Néman.

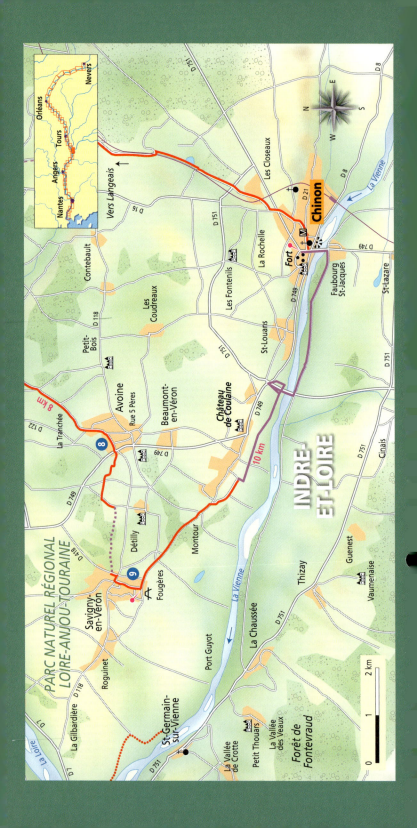

## Stage 11 / From Langeais to Chinon

◆ The faultless signposting continues along a small traffic-free road to the pleasant village of **Avoine**.

❽ From there, a series of cyclist-only trails and short shared sections lead to the neighbouring village of **Savigny-en-Véron**.

❾ In Savigny-en-Véron, turn left at the village square to join a series of shared small roads and cyclist-only paths to **Chinon** via Montour and **the banks of the River Vienne**. The only problem with this option (compared to the more direct – but rougher route which you could take earlier in Huismes) is that it imposes an additional fifteen kilo-

*An unmissable stage: the fortress of Chinon.*

metre trip! It is up to you to decide whether it is possible depending on your tour plans, the time you have available and the route and terrain which suit you best.

◆ A third option is still possible for those who find themselves short of time and who need to start making their way back as soon as possible. When leaving

**Savigny-en-Véron**, an 8 km path which is just as well signposted as the first two, allows you to head north to the Loire and the bridge leading to **Port-Boulet**. The SNCF railway station provides transport to Orléans, Tours, Saumur and Angers. Pure magic!

*The Indre at its confluence.*

## Stage 12
# From Chinon to Saumur

**35 km**

› A stage with incomparable treasures between two regions, Touraine and Anjou. But also between two wines: Chinon on the slopes of the Vienne (much appreciated by Rabelais it is said) and Le saumur-Champigny, a prestigious red wine from the south bank of the Loire.... After leaving Chinon, its castle and vineyards, the first village you come to is the picture postcard Candes-Saint-Martin (opposite) situated at the confluence of the Vienne and the Loire. This is followed by Montsoreau, which offers the opportunity for an excursion to Fontevraud Abbey, and, finally, Turquant, with its vineyards and wineries just before the magnificent town of Saumur.

## Stage 12 / From Chinon to Saumur

### Chinon in brief

Set on the right bank of the Vienne about fifteen kilometres from its confluence with the Loire, the Rabelaisian town of Chinon is at its best when seen from the opposite bank, which is how *Loire à vélo* tourists arrive along the recommended route! It offers a wide view over the river, the town and the lacework of the towers and the ruined walls which are all that remains of Milieu Castle.

If you have the time, stop at the Maison de la Rivière: in the past, Chinon played a leading role on the inland waterways.

Then climb up to the castle (Tel:02 47 93 13 45). A visit to its fortified wall, towers and its restored dwellings is well worth it. La Tour de Boissy, among others, offers an outstanding view over Chinon and its valley.

At dinner, enjoy a glass of Chinon, a wine which the members of the local confrérie – the Bons Entonneurs Rabelaisiens – are always more than happy to promote.

*Animated museum of wine and barrel-making,*
*Tel: 02 47 93 25 63*
*12, rue Voltaire, 37500 Chinon*

*Tourist office:*
*Place Hofheim,*
*37500 Chinon*
*Tel: 02 47 93 17 85*
*www.chinon-valdeloire.com*

### Candes in confluence

Today, Candes is listed as one of the "most beautiful villages in France" and, for many years, has been a major river port at the crossroads of freight traffic along the Vienne and the Loire. It has also been a witness to, or a victim of, many legendary spates: here and there, plaques offer reminders of the different "historical" levels reached by the combined waters of the two rivers.

*and the only viewpoint from which it is possible to photograph or film Candes and the neighbouring Montsoreau Castle from their best angles!*

**Note**
→ *a modernised toue –*
*L'Amarante – at the entrance to the village offers the opportunity to enjoy a "local" excursion or cruise, including at sunset. Do not miss the trip: it is one of the only times of the day,*

*L'Amarante cruise boat,*
*Tel:02 47 95 80 85*
*and 06 33 34 57 16*

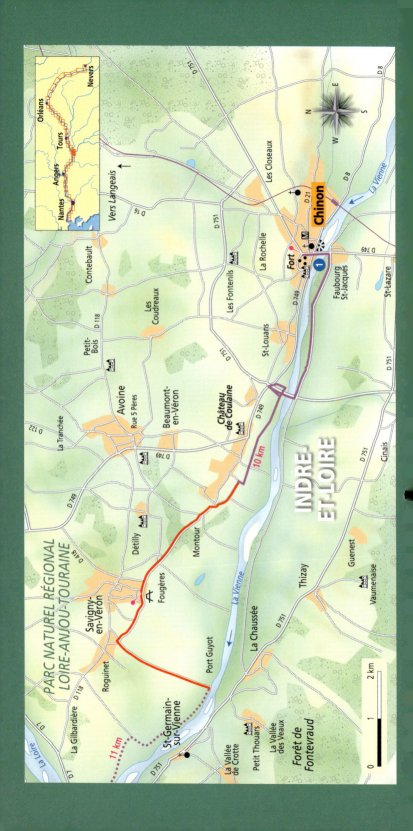

Stage 12 / From Chinon to Saumur

## View of the slopes

◆ Be careful! Although the first part of the day's stage is flat and comfortable, the section after Turquet is one of the only hilly sections on the *Loire à vélo* trail. Remember to take a break.

❶ Between Chinon and Candes, the confluence of the Loire and the Vienne is a nerve centre. This is great because the paths in the sector are comfortable, well-surfaced, shaded, and secure. Follow the **banks of the Vienne** to Montour and then continue to Savigny-en-Véron.

◆ After **Savigny-en-Véron**, all the paths come together on their way to **Candes** meaning that you will be following cyclist-only paths and small, quiet roads.

*Opposite Candes-Saint-Martin, the Vienne joins the Loire.*

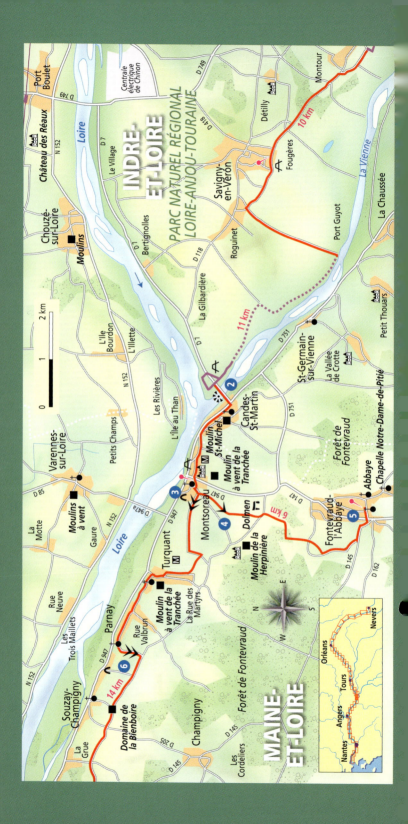

## Stage 12 / From Chinon to Saumur

*Spoilt for choice.*

② At the panoramic bridge on arrival in **Candes-Saint-Martin**, there is a stunning view over the site: the village of Candes, the wide River Vienne which flows past its base and, slightly further on, the confluence of this river with the Loire.

◆ Be careful not to be too distracted by the view because the bridge has no cycle path! If you want to enjoy or film the view, it is best to leave your bicycle behind and follow the footpath.

③ Montsoreau Castle is a short distance from Candes-Saint-Martin. This "decorative" fortress immortalised by Alexander Dumas and his "Dame de Montsoreau" is well worth a visit (Tel: 02 41 67 12 60).

④ A detour by **Fontevraud**? The cycle path which leads to the abbey from the exit of Monstereau is a must, despite the 12 km round-trip and a few (small) hills. But how could you even consider getting this far without visiting it?

⑤ The answer is visible over the top of your handlebars: one of the most beautiful abbeys in the world is well worth a few extra kilometres.

◆ In Montsoreau, continue towards **Saumur**. The evening's stopover is just 15 km away! This temporary section of the *Loire à vélo* trail has plenty of attractions. There is a small hill when leaving Montsoreau before a major climb (18%) at **Parnay**, but, nothing prevents you from walking up it if you want!

*Parnay Church.*

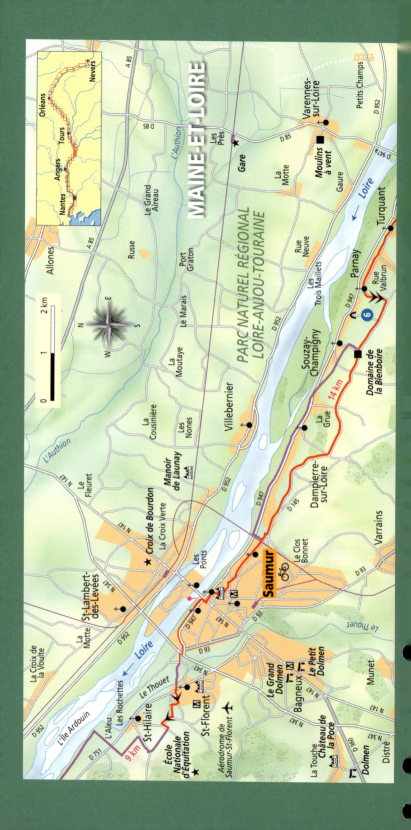

## Stage 12 / From Chinon to Saumur

*The Clos-Cristal in Souzay-Champigny.*

❻ The two or three hills along the route are never very long and allow you to progress, without too much effort, through a beautiful environment of slopes covered with appellation controlee vineyards. In the heart of Saumur-Champigny, between vineyards and villages built in tufa, you will pass through **Turquant** first of all,

*Saumur and its castle from the Loire à vélo viewpoint.*

◆ The *Loire à vélo* trail now offers you the opportunity to travel to **Saumur** directly along the riverside. However, having said that, the

"wine" variant is far from being uninteresting. After a short hill at Parnay, it does not alter its hillside route until it reaches the castle. A final stop on the street overlooking the Loire and its huge sand banks on the right and you will find yourself at the terrace-viewpoint which collapsed relatively recently but which now shows a renewed air of confidence. If you decide not to visit these sites straightaway, the shared route of the *Loire à vélo* trail invites you to freewheel (carefully) down the bypass ramp to the town centre.

**Not to be missed,**
→ the cave site of *La Grande Vignole, Turquant*, Tel: 02 41 38 16 44
Demonstration of "pommes tapées" famous in the Angers region. Parnay, Tel: 02 41 51 48 30

*Excursion*
# Fontevraud Abbey

**12 km**

Anjou Departmental Tourist Board

› In the same way as it offers a wealth of historic homes, the Valley of the Kings also offers a large number of prestigious sanctuaries. Cathedrals, churches, chapels and abbeys sometimes lie a few kilometres from the river, but are always easy to access by bicycle tourists. Without a doubt, Fontevraud Abbey is one of the most flamboyant examples, with its recently restored buildings and its famous polychrome recumbent statues. Situated less than half an hour's ride from Montsoreau, it is one of the jewels of the *Loire à vélo* trail, so why miss it?

## Fontevraud in brief

Ph. Anjou Departmental Tourist Board

One of the most beautiful sites on the Loire, the construction of Fontevraud royal abbey started in the 12th century and was completed in the 18th century. It was at that time – and still is – the largest monastic building in Western Christendom: 14 ha! Abandoned and turned into a prison between the Revolution and the second half of the 20th century, the abbey has come a long way since those days. Now more beautiful than ever, it has been the stage for one of the largest restoration projects of the past few decades…
Do not miss a visit to the huge abbey as well as the cloisters and Saint-Benoît and Saint-Lazare chapels… not to mention, above all, the Romanesque kitchens, a round building measuring 30 m high from which it is said that 3,000 meals could be served.

*Fontevraud royal abbey,*
*Tel: 02 41 51 71 41*

*Tourist office:*
*Place Saint-Michel,*
*49590 Fontevraud-l'Abbaye*
*Tel: 02 41 51 79 45*

## Mystical detour

◆ From Montsoreau, you will be able to reach the abbey by following the highly visible official waymarking.

◆ Climbing slightly at the southwest exit of the town, the route is almost completely free of traffic. Therefore, no safety concerns, you just need enough energy to press down on the pedals and climb the few hills and rises which are a result of the Angevin topography. Since leaving Montsoreau, we have now arrived in Maine-et-Loire!

◆ The recommended route passes the edge of Fontevraud forest and provides access to the top of the village which has taken its name from the abbey. You will then descend to the entrance of the monastic building, which may be entered with your bicycle: a special parking area has been created for cyclists within the building's walls!

◆ After your visit, the return trip is just as easy. Although you will have to make up any of the altitude you may have lost, the road to Montsoreau is mainly downhill. Just before the village, do not forget to turn left at the signpost! You will find yourself back on the *Loire à vélo* trail to Saumur.

## Stage 13
# From Saumur to Gennes

**19 km**

> A short and peaceful stage which will allow you plenty of time to visit the castle and the lively streets of old Saumur before departing. You will then be able to enjoy the charm of a riverside route which reflects the gentle pace of life in the region of Angers. The departmental road situated between the two cyclist-only stretches, fortunately, has been "tamed", encouraging you to make a few epicurean stops along the riverbank and at the welcoming villages which bask in the riverside sunlight. After this, a good idea for a picnic is a detour, just before Gennes, into the forest set on the shores of a lake, one of the most beautiful rest areas along the length of the Loire route. So, make the most of it!

## Stage 13 / From Saumur to Gennes

## Saumur in brief

A major tourist centre, the "jewel of Anjou" lives in the shadow of its prestigious castle, with horses and wine as its symbols. Everywhere references to the local wines Saumur and Saumur-Champigny are visible, and it is astonishing that there are not more references to the cavalry. After visiting the famous castle of the Dukes of Anjou (Tel: 02 41 40 24 40), which is already home to the Horse Museum, pay a visit to the Ecole nationale d'Equitation and its famous Cadre Noir (Tel: 02 41 53 50 60). There, you will discover the history of the French Cavalry School, see the horses of the Cadre Noir, watch them in training and, at certain dates, enjoy some of the displays which have made their reputation. Plan this visit for when you are leaving the town because the school is in Saint-Hilaire-Saint-Florent, west of Saumur, on the route you will take downstream towards Gennes and Angers.

In the meantime, take the time to lose yourself in the winding streets of the old town (more than 50 listed buildings!). Perhaps you will find a little of the atmosphere from the novel Eugénie Grandet by Balzac.

In terms of the river, here the Loire is much wider than it appears at first sight. Cross the old Pont Cessart, and enjoy the view over Offard Island on the way, and then cross a second bridge which passes over a different branch of the river in order to access the right bank (SNCF railway station and bicycle hire nearby: "Détours de Loire").

### Also, in Saumur, do not miss

→ The Gratien & Meyer winery (Tel: 02 41 83 13 30) at the exit of the town on the road to Montsoreau. Dug out of the tufa in the Middle Ages, it is a beautiful example of winemaking know-how in Saumur. Wine-tasting available.

→ The Musée des Blindés, route de Fontevraud (Tel: 02 41 83 69 90). Related to the cavalry – and, therefore, to Saumur – and tanks, a collection may be seen here which is unique in the world, with more than 200 tanks, armoured vehicles and artillery.

→ Le Saumur-Loire boat cruise (Tel: 02 41 53 65 33). Moored at a jetty just in front of the town hall all summer long, this modernised toue is able to carry up to 60 people for mini cruises (50 minutes) on its way past and around Saumur. Ideal for photographing the town and its castle from their best angles!

**Tourist office:
Place de la Bilange,
49400 Saumur
Tel: 02 41 40 20 60**

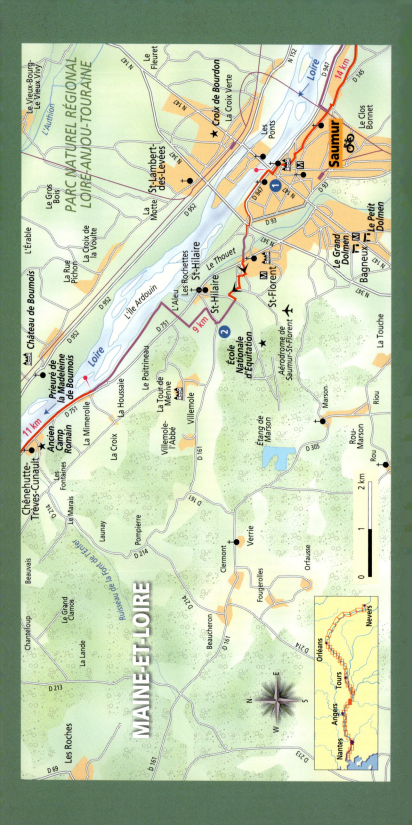

*Stage 13* / From Saumur to Gennes

# The private side of the Loire

**❶** When leaving by the old historical bridge in Saumur (**Pont Cessart** leading to Offard Island and the right bank of the Loire), the *Loire à vélo* trail is far from peaceful, but it does provide a good protected cycle path as far as **Saint-Florent**.

◆ Be careful not to miss the cyclist-only stretch which follows,100 m further on (towards McDonald's) which allows you to safely bypass the large roundabout on the N 147!

*Saumur, view of Pont Cessart.*

**❷** Follow the waymarking closely and share the road for a short while in the upper reaches of **Saint-Hilaire**, (steep climb) before returning back down to the river. After that, the *Loire à vélo* trail offers one of its sumptuous riverside sections of which only it knows the secret.

*The Loire from the top of the town.*

◆ A few stunning (and refreshing thanks to the well-shaded path) kilometres along an environmentally-friendly road surface - it is a pity having to join the **D 751** to reach **Cunault**, but, fortunately, it is not a very busy road and great efforts have been made to ensure the safety of its users.

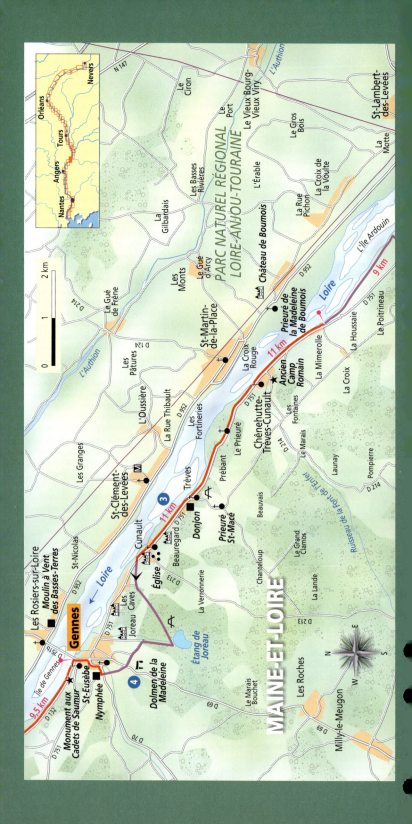

## Stage 13 / From Saumur to Gennes

③ Between Cunault and Gennes, almost without warning, the Loire à vélo trail chooses **Cunault** to leave the banks of the Loire, which it has followed for the past twelve kilometres. However, no regrets, because although it does involve a steep climb, this is only in order to offer you the opportunity to enjoy an outstanding greenway.

④ It winds its way through a forest to **Joreau Lake** and the picnic stop which may be found there. If you have left Saumur a little late, this is an ideal lunch stop with the site of the lake, a well-maintained nature reserve, providing a haven of peace. Still traffic-free, the greenway then passes near the **dolmen of La Madeleine** (this part of the Loire has a large number of megaliths) before dipping down into Gennes.

## Medieval stopovers

Peaceful stopovers, Chênehutte, Trèves and Cunault are beacons of the local heritage with their old stones, tufa walls and cave galleries... Above all, do not miss the churches of Notre-Dame in Chênehutte and of Saint-Aubin in Trèves, as well as a stop at the foot of the famous keep in Trèves opposite: 30 m high, the only remains of the fortress built here in the 15th century by Robert LeMaçon, a local baron and comrade in arms of Joan of Arc! In Cunault, where there is still a boule de fort society (a sort of Angevin bowling game played on a curved pitch), do not miss a visit to the Romanesque church - with its square 11th century bell tower and its 223 capitals, it is one of the most beautiful Romanesque buildings in Anjou.

## Stage 14
# From Gennes to Angers

**42 km**

> A rather long stage, but one without any particular difficulties in terms of the terrain… apart from a few kilometres climb to the top of Angers! An old abbey (Saint-Maur), Saint-Rémy-la-Varenne, Saint-Mathurin, and La Daguenière are the "curiosities" along a route which, no longer able to follow the right bank of the river, makes an incursion into the reclaimed landscapes of the Loire-Anjou-Touraine regional nature park. From La Daguenière to the centre of Angers, the final bends of this section run through the strange landscapes of the former slate quarries in Trélazé.

*Etape 14* / From Gennes to Angers

## Gennes in brief

In logistical terms, Gennes is a welcome stopover. Situated between the two major tourist centres of Saumur and Angers, it is a sort of rest stopover where you are able to gather your strength. Take full advantage of what this site has to offer: a mild "angevin" climate, peace and quiet, and a relaxing pace of life. In terms of heritage, pay a visit to the Gallo-Roman ruins of an amphitheatre, an aqueduct and baths as well as the remains of Saint-Eusèbe Church (10th century doorway), Saint-Vétérin Church (12th-13th centuries) and Sarré watermill (16th century), one of the last still operating in the region situated southwest of the village on a small tributary of the Loire.

*Gennois Tourist Office:*
*Place de l'Etoile, 49350 Gennes*
*Tel: 02 41 51 84 14*

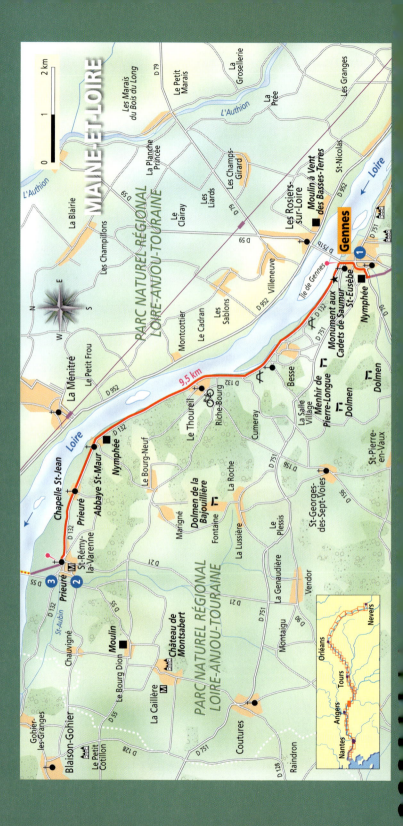

## Etape 14 / From Gennes to Angers

*Saint-Maur Abbey.*

## Hello Anjou!

**1** There is a large choice of rest areas along this stage so plan a picnic for lunch! The "official" *Loire à vélo* trail obliges you to share the first part of the route for about ten kilometres.

◆ **On the left bank, the D 132** practically runs along the length of the river offering superb and untamed viewpoints particularly on the stretch between **Le Thoureil** and **the Abbey of Saint-Maur**.

**2** No reserved path before **Saint-Rémy-la-Varenne**, but after that, a cyclist-only path offers the comfort and safety of a shortcut as far as **Saint-Mathurin bridge**. Cross the bridge only after visiting **Saint-Rémy**: with its 12th century Benedictine priory, paved streets and intimate town centre, the village is well worth the detour!

*The bridge in Saint-Mathurin-sur-Loire, sadly without a reserved path.*

**3** Retrace your steps a little to the **east of Saint-Rémy** and join the short (but much appreciated) cycle path to the Loire and the **Saint-Mathurin Bridge**. When you arrive at the bridge, do not attempt to climb the staircase but ride around the bridge's pier. Go to the snack bar-restaurant which enjoys a clear view over the Loire and the bridge and then cross the road on to the right-hand pavement.

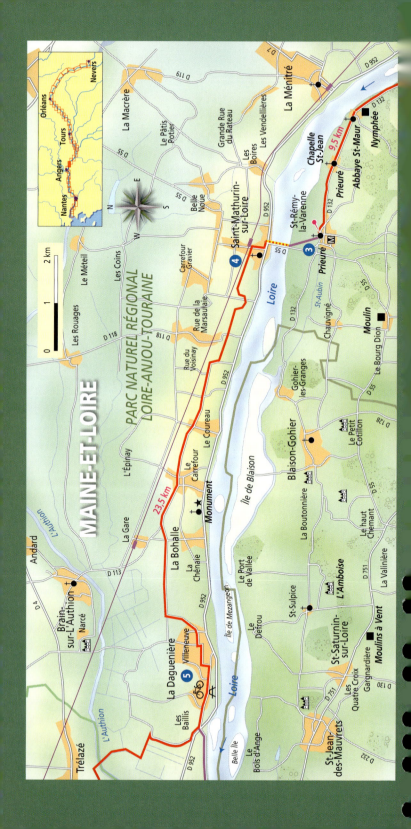

## Etape 14 / From Gennes to Angers

◆ Be careful, the **bridge in Saint-Mathurin** does not have a reserved path, therefore, it is best to cross it on foot if you want to avoid the traffic and the risk of riding along the narrow pavement. However, the bridge is the only way you are able to cross to the right bank.

❹ When leaving **Saint-Mathurin** (right bank of the river), the landscape is very different from what you have been seeing on the left bank since Saumur and Gennes. The *Loire à vélo* trail is very different too and, for obvious safety reasons, avoids the very busy riverside levee to join a cycle path which loses itself in the neighbouring marshland.

◆ But, there is no risk of getting lost along this temporary route which cuts an erratic path through the river's former meanders. If the occasional tufa houses with their slate roofs were not there to remind you that you are still in the Val de Loire, it would be easy to believe that you are in Flanders! Be sure to take a look at the river which is very wide here in the regional nature park in La Daguenière.

❺ At **La Daguenière,** the D952 leaves the Loire on its way to Angers. This is fortunate because it leaves behind a large cyclist-only section (the levee which the departmental road has left) at least as far as Ponts-de-Cé. It is ideal for

### Saint-Mathurin-sur-Loire in brief

Former port and stage post between Saumur and Angers, Saint-Mathurin – as much as Saint-Rémy-la-Varenne – provides the opportunity for a well-deserved break for cyclists, among other things for its "Maison de la Loire en Anjou", its museum, completely redesigned in 2007, which presents everything you need to know about the river: the water, the people, the sand, the landscapes, the fauna and the flora.

*Maison de la Loire,
place Charles-Cigogne,
Tel: 02 41 57 37 55*

*Loire-Authion Tourist office:
Place du Port-Charles-Sigogne,
49250 Saint-Martin-sur-Loire
Tel: 02 41 57 01 82*

a peaceful rediscovery of the river as you ride beneath the welcoming shade of the large poplars. And, all this in complete safety!

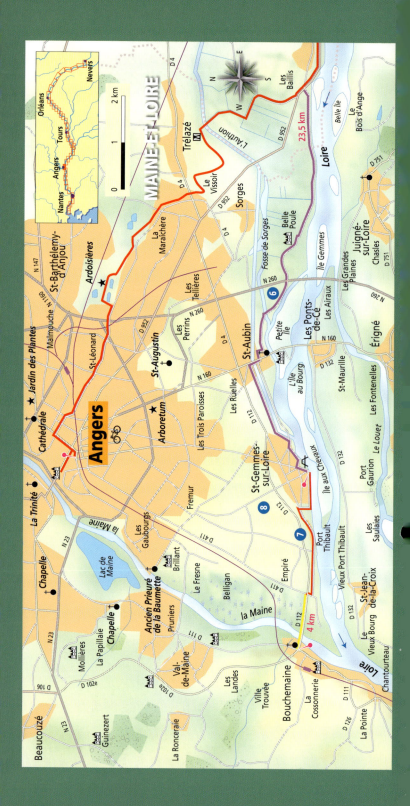

## Etape 14 / From Gennes to Angers

⑥ The famous **Ponts-de-Cé** is the only place where the position of the islands and the layout of the branches of the Loire allowed bridges to be built between two banks.

◆ The *Loire à vélo* trail only crosses two of them. The first over the Authion, just before **Saint-Aubin**, and the second over its side canal, which you will follow along a cyclist-only section as far as the pretty village of **Sainte-Gemmes-sur-Loire** and its **Belle Rive promenade**. There are just a few kilometres left before Bouchemaine Bridge and the attractive stopover on the right bank of the Maine.

## A new slate path to reach Angers

⑦ The new eastern access route to Angers through the slate quarries of Trélazé starts by crossing the Authion via a small ferry.

⑧ You will then pass through the astonishing former slate quarry in a landscape of blue schist and old mines transformed into lakes. A visit to the Slate Museum is a must.

*Tél. 02 41 69 04 71*
*www.lemuseedelardoise.fr*

## Stage 15
# From Angers to Montjean

**40 km**

> A superb stage which starts by following the banks of the River Maine before reaching the Loire – at the appropriately named Bouchemaine – which you left behind in Sainte-Gemmes, at the end of the previous stage. This is the Loire of fishermen and sailors and the cycle path will encounter the evidence and remains of their presence throughout the day, starting with Savennières and Béhuard Island situated opposite it. The route continues via Possonnière and Chalonnes-sur-Loire, which used to be a major port when sailing boats provided the main source of trade, before, at the end of the stage, following a cycle path from one end of Chalonnes Island to the other and arriving on the formerly very active quaysides of the river port of Montjean.

## Stage 15 / From Angers to Montjean

## Angers in brief

With almost 150 km of cycle paths and a clearly affirmed green policy, Angers is one of the great modern cities of high environmental quality. Coming from La Daguenière and the slate quarries of Trélazé (see previous page), access to the upper part of the city is the only (small) difficulty at the end of the stage. Start by visiting the castle, ideally situated opposite the Tourist office (find out about the City-Pass while you are there!), or rather we should say the fortress, with its one thousand-year history, its 17 huge towers, its moat-gardens and interior treasures: dwellings and chapels, covered way and gallery of the Apocalypse. Against the southern wall, it houses a genuine medieval cartoon strip (76 prints over 100 m of tapestries dating from the 14th century) inspired by the visions of Saint John. When leaving the castle, do not miss the sweeping view to the west over the Maine and the opposite "town" of La Doutre. This lower (floodable) neighbourhood of Angers, thus named from the term "d'outre Maine" (from outside Maine), has been the major construction project in Angers in recent years. We will be going there later on the downstream *Loire à vélo* trail.

In the meantime there is plenty to do, starting with the nearby Saint-Maurice Cathedral and the view – over the River Maine still – from the "Montée Saint-Maurice". You may continue the visit with Place Sainte-Croix, Rue Chaperonnière and Place du Ralliement, as far as Place du Pilori. Along the way, do not miss the famous Maison d'Adam (16th century). There are also two other unmissable visits: Saint-Martin collegiate church (in the street of the same name), recently and magnificently restored by the Maine-et-Loire departmental council, and the famous David d'Angers gallery, which you will stumble upon as you make your way back to the castle. Established in the nave of an old abbey, it presents the works (busts, statues, medallions and monumental reproductions) of the sculptor David d'Angers (1788–1856).

*Greater Angers tourist office:*
*7, place Kennedy*
*(opposite the castle)*
*Tel: 02 41 23 50 00*
*Website:*
*www.angersloiretourisme.com*

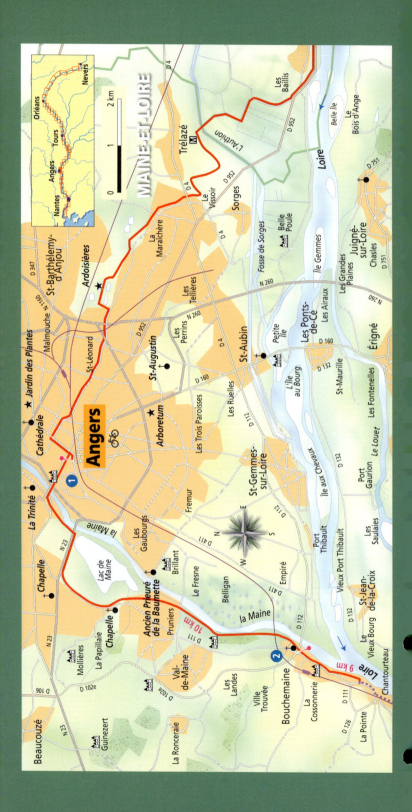

*Stage 15* / From Angers to Montjean

## Along the water

**❶** After crossing **Pont de la Basse-Chaîne**, at the foot of Angers castle (along the way, do not miss the Hôtel du Roi de Pologne), you will have to pass part of the new residential neighbourhood of **La Doutre** to enter the huge **Parc du Maine** (250 ha). This floodable Angers version of "Central Park" surrounds a large interior lake and you will have to follow its shores towards **Bouchemaine**. Shortly after the large camp site, take the metal footbridge on the right. On the left, you will skirt the lake and arrive back in Angers...

*Picnic area, wide angle view of the confluence of the River Maine and the River Loire.*

◆ Until its confluence with the Loire, the few kilometres along the banks of the Maine are delightful and are all the more enjoyable because the route has only recently been opened after being damaged by the frequent spates.

**❷** After crossing a metal bridge reserved for pedestrians and cyclists, and then a rail bridge, the path arrives at the stopover and **road bridge of Bouchemaine**. The confluence lies slightly beyond this at **La Pointe**. Do not forget to

*A guaranteed clear view.*

take a break for a little photography before choosing the next stage of the route to follow.

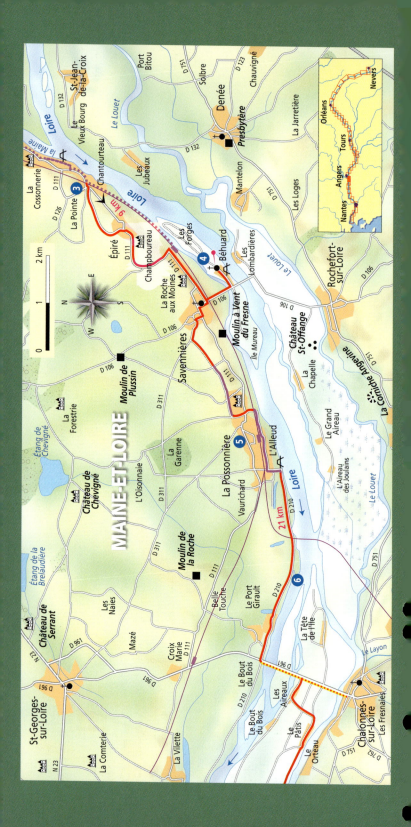

## Stage 15 / From Angers to Montjean

# At the mercy of the river

◆ The Loire's moods will often force you to travel to **Savennières**, via **Epiré**, along the interior route. This is feasible, although there is a slight hill and you will have to share a few kilometres of road with the sometimes unpredictable road traffic. However, it is also interesting because you are in the heart of the **Savennières** appellation and the famous **Coulée-de-Serrant** from Château de la Roche-aux-Moines (an outstanding white wine) is nearby.

❸ But, if the waters of the Loire are not too high, the new route is much more pleasant. It follows a small path along the river to the stopovers of **La Pointe** and then **Savennières**. The final section, shared by both options, runs along the railway line to just below Savennières and the bridge leading to **Béhuard Island**.

❹ Do not miss an island excursion! There, you will discover the unusual church, which, according to legend, was built on a rock by Louis XI to thank the heavens for having saved him from shipwreck.

❺ There are also two other options possible for getting from Savennières to **La Possonnière**. Follow the "interior" waymarking

for the *Loire à vélo* trail which leads up to the top of the village along a small traffic-free and flat route. Or, if the water level allows it, follow the riverside to the bottom of La Possonnière.

◆ A beautiful reconstruction of an old-style river port awaits you. The site has a number of traditional Loire boats which you may watch in action on the water, including some under sail, as soon as the fine weather arrives.

◆ A delightful place for a midday break (or for a night: the neighbouring municipal camp site is particularly welcome), the snack bar and the terrace of the port of La

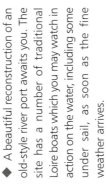

*The river port of La Possonnière.*

Possonnière, one of the most intimate and charming sites on the route.

❻ The danger-free levee which follows the **D 210** does not offer any shade until **Port-Girault** and Pont de **Chalonnes**, 5 km further on! Therefore, be careful of the heat in the summer months.

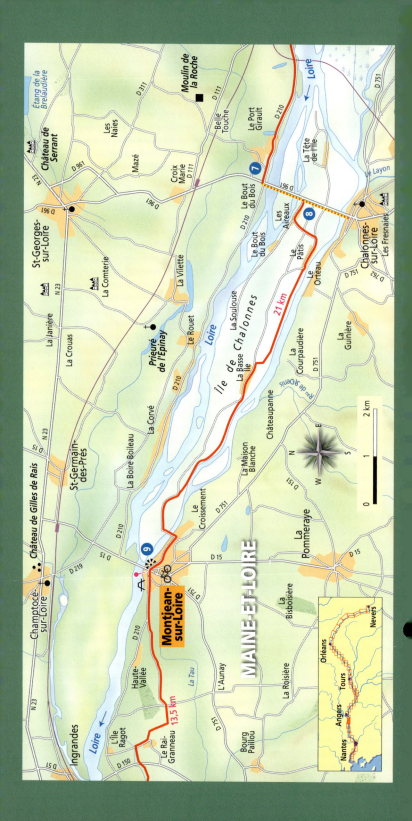

## Stage 15 / From Angers to Montjean

**7** Be careful when arriving at **Chalonnes Bridge** and when you are crossing it. Although it has been secured, the cycle path which runs alongside the road is dangerous.

◆ Unless you are running late, on the right, after the first bridge, do not hesitate to enjoy the entire bridge crossing (2 km!) and continue to **Chalonnes**.

**8** After visiting the town, cross the southern part of the bridge again… and return to the waymarking for the *Loire à vélo* trail. Comprising small, traffic-free asphalt roads protected by large trees, the route provides perfect peace as far as **Montjean**. It runs along the entire length of the island to which Chalonnes gave its name: the longest island on the course of the Loire (11 km)!

*The port of Chalonnes, a former river port of prime importance.*

**9** At the very end of the island, a footbridge provides access to the former river port of Montjean, after passing the almost medieval remains of the old bridge over the river towards Champtocé (and Saint-Germain-des-Prés).

*Old Loire sailing boats.*

## Stage 16
# From Montjean to Oudon-Champtoceaux 38 km

> The day's route winds its way through the lowlands of the left bank. It only returns to the river at Saint-Florent-le-Vieil and Ancenis! Therefore, it is quite a long stage, but one which is quiet and comfortable. It is also particularly rich in historical reminders and poetic reminiscences: War in the Vendée and the last fishermen of the Loire in Saint-Florent-le-Vieil, Joachim du Bellay in Liré-sous-Ancenis, reminders of ancient battles in Oudon.... All of this set in an abundance of islands, boires (secondary branches), groynes and sandbanks which the river plays with as the waters rise and fall.

## Stage 16 / From Montjean to Oudon-Champtoceaux

## Montjean-sur-Loire in brief

Safe at the extremity of the long island of Chalonnes, Montjean (pronounced "Montejean"!) was for many years a passing place over the Loire, and, above all, a major river port. Although its traditional quaysides provide proof of this ancient activity, it is difficult to imagine that, in the 18th century, more than 12,000 boats stopped here every year.
Complete your visit with a mini cruise on the Loire. La Montjeannaise, a well-named gabarre, provides a subtle and skilful demonstration of navigation on this downstream section of the last untamed river in Europe.

*Tourist Office:*
*rue d'Anjou*
*Tel: 02 41 39 07 10*
*www.montjean.net*

*Cruises aboard the gabarre La Montjeannaise, information from the tourist office.*

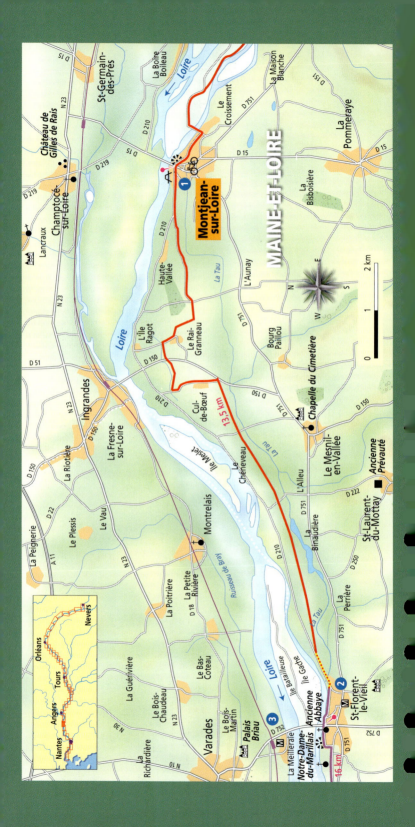

*Stage 16* / From Montjean to Oudon-Champtoceaux

# A leisurely route

**❶** Departing from the bridge in Montjean, the *Loire à vélo* trail follows the left bank "levee" for just a few hundred metres.

◆ Its temporary route then leads immediately down below it through fields and grassland. A small, traffic-free asphalt road then follows, but for the 13km journey to **Saint-Florent-le-Vieil**, you will no longer see the Loire, its islands, or its neighbouring villages (especially Le Fresne and Ingrandes, the two twin villages which, on the opposite banks, stretch along the waterside for 2 km)!

Ph. Anjou Departmental Tourist Board

**❷** You will have to wait until the outskirts of **Saint-Florent-le-Vieil** and the passage over the D 210 for an attractive cyclist-only route in order to return to the water and access directly the paved quaysides of the lower town.

**❸** A pity that the double bridge in **Saint-Florent** has such a lot of traffic (you will have to use the pavement) because it is from the opposite shore, on the right bank, that you will have the best view over the entire site and, more precisely, from the quayside lined with hollyhocks in the old Loire fishermen's neighbourhood: **La Meilleraie**. The flat-bottomed boats and other Loire vessels are still there… and a few old fishermen are always willing to tell you about their lives and what their river used to be like.

## Stage 16 / From Montjean to Oudon-Champtoceaux

## The river's highs and lows

It is difficult to imagine that the indolent or impetuous river that you can see today, almost completely free of navigation, used to be so busy over the centuries and seasons. For many years exploited and used in accordance – whether consciously or not – with its ecological balance, the river has suffered a great deal from the industrial era. The abusive extraction of its sand, excessive scouring and dragging of its estuary (to allow increasingly large boats to sail as far as Nantes) have had disastrous effects, with, among other things, erosion of the riverbanks. This has lead mainly to the widening of the riverbed and a paradoxical increase in the number and surface area of the sandbanks which lead the waters astray during the dry season...

It is a lesson for which the Loire is going to have to pay a heavy price. Apparently, more than a century will be needed for nature and the natural movement of the waters to return the river to its original state.

## Stage 16 / From Montjean to Oudon-Champtoceaux

### Saint-Florent-le-Vieil

Perched on a rocky schist outcrop, Saint-Florent was a centre of the War in the Vendée; the small museum which occupies the old Chapel of the Sacré-Cœur recounts the tragic story. In the huge strategic movement (the "virée de Galerne") undertaken by the Vendean army in autumn 1793, tens of thousands of men, women and children were forced to cross the Loire here… and were massacred a few weeks later by the Republican troops. The best solution for accessing the building (and the view it offers over the river and the opposite shore), is to leave your bicycle at the bottom, on Quai de la Gabelle for example. This name, meaning salt tax, is very appropriate, since the sector was renowned for many long years for salt smuggling. Salt was very rare and heavily taxed at that time and was as much as ten times cheaper in La Meilleraie, the Breton village on the right bank!

*Tourist office:*
*4, place de la Février,*
*49410 Saint-Florent-le-Vieil*
*Tel: 02 41 72 62 32*

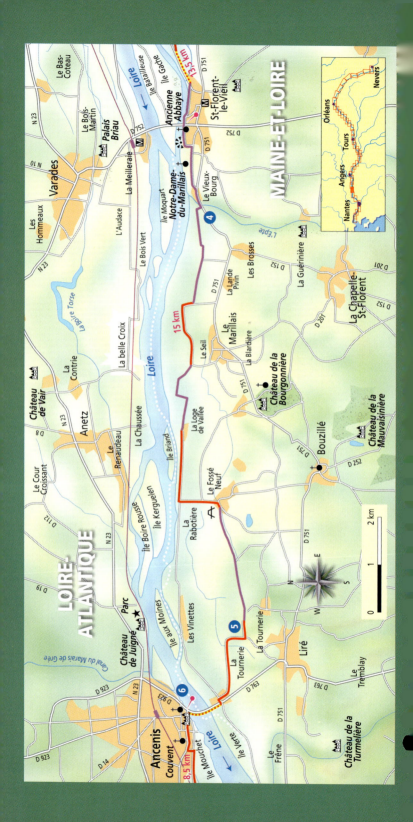

## stage 16 / From Montjean to Oudon-Champtoceaux

◆ Just after **the bridge in Saint-Florent** – which, fortunately you will cross from **Quai de la Gabelle** – marks the start of an attractive stabilised reinforced path (to protect it from spates) which makes its way between the promontory of the upper town and the river to the church of **Notre-Dame-du-Marillais** and the small village alongside it.

approach to **Le Fossé-Neuf**, where you will be able to enjoy a huge picnic area.

**5** Do not miss the opportunity for a pilgrimage to the neighbouring village – Liré – the nostalgic base for Joachim du Bellay, less then 1 km south of the *Loire à vélo* trail...

◆ Those in a hurry will take the direct route from Ancenis via **Le Fourneau**. In all cases, along the way, it is impossible to avoid the shared passage on the access ramp and over the bridge leading to Ancenis on the right bank.

**4** Cross the river of Julien Gracq – the Epte – on which you may enjoy a boat or canoe excursion. Then, in an environment of bocage meadows and cereal crops, a combination of cyclist-only routes and small traffic-free roads lead you back to the Loire, majestic on its

## Ancenis in brief

Grouped together around its fortified castle (the site used to serve as a military "bolt" on the Loire between Brittany and Anjou), the old town of Ancenis pays a legitimate and well deserved tribute to Du Bellay. To the left of the bridge coming from his "petit Liré" do not miss the statue of the famous poet.

*"[...] Plus me plaît le séjour
qu'ont bâti mes aïeux
Que des palais romains les fronts audacieux
Plus que le marbre dur me plaît l'ardoise fine
Plus mon petit Liré que le mont Palatin...
Et plus que l'air marin la douceur angevine"*

Ancenis castle may well be closed temporarily for restoration work, but that does not prevent you from admiring the watchtower and the two towers of the entrance bastion. Also pay a visit to the town and why not make the most of a lunch break: the town has some good restaurants offering Loire specialities and vintage wines (Coteaux d'Ancennis and Malvoisie). Authentic country-style market on Thursday mornings.

**Tourist office:
27, rue du Château,
44150 Ancenis
Tel: 02 40 83 07 44**

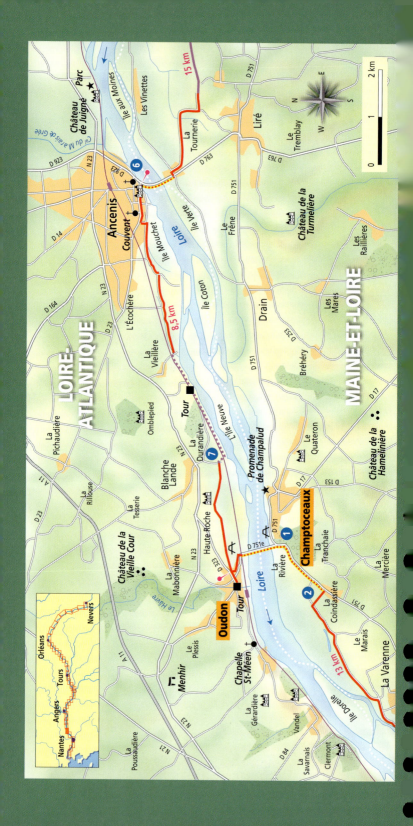

## Stage 16 / From Montjean to Oudon-Champtoceaux

*The tower-keep in Oudon.*

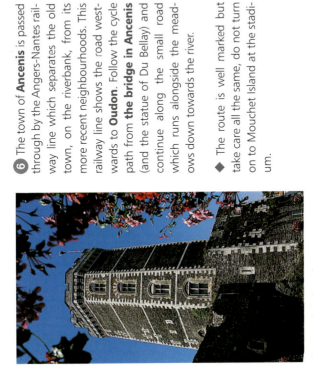

*Greenway in Oudon.*

**6** The town of **Ancenis** is passed through by the Angers-Nantes railway line which separates the old town, on the riverbank, from its more recent neighbourhoods. This railway line shows the road westwards to **Oudon**. Follow the cycle path from **the bridge in Ancenis** (and the statue of Du Bellay) and continue along the small road which runs alongside the meadows down towards the river.

◆ The route is well marked but take care all the same, do not turn on to Mouchet Island at the stadium.

◆ Continue for slightly more than 3 km and stay close to the railway line Angers-Nantes.

**7** At **Pont-Moricaud**, turn right as if to pass below the railway line. Turn left before it and follow the stony but comfortable path **to Oudon** (about 6 km) between the rail embankment and the Loire.

◆ A flat and easy route alongside the river until the route passes to the other side of the railway line via a large picnic area near the village. Continue either straight ahead to **Oudon**, or turn left to **Champtoceaux**, via the bridge over the Loire. Unfortunately there is no cycle path!

## Stage 17
# From Oudon-Champtoceaux to Nantes  30 km

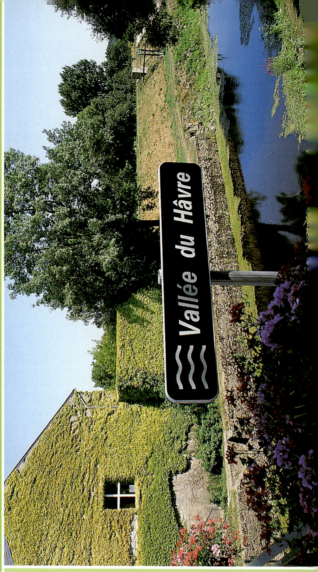

▸ To reach Mauves and the Nantes road, the *Loire à vélo* trail could have opted for the easy solution contenting itself with continuing straight from Oudon between the river and the railway line. Fortunately, it has chosen the other solution along the south bank. Before the bridge in Mauves, you will have time to admire the "great wall" of La Divatte, a huge levee protecting the market gardens from flooding. Back on the right bank, the cycle path is completely straight as far as Nantes, which, before the city's suburbs, offers long sections along the riverside which is now subject to the rhythms of the tides.

## Stage 17 / From Oudon-Champtoceaux to Nantes

## Oudon in brief

The star of the show in the small town of Oudon is the tower which dominates its western part, providing a reminder of its fierce defensive past. Although you will have to climb a small slope in order to get to it, be sure not to miss a visit to this fortified keep built in the 14th century on a rocky outcrop overlooking the Loire (facing the cliff on the opposite shore on which stands the village of Champtoceaux): the octagonal tower offers a spectacular view over the region and, inside, is completed by a historical presentation combined with a virtual balloon flight over the Loire. Also, take the time to ride down to the small SNCF railway station and the neighbouring marina.

Here, with their groynes and sandbanks, the banks of the river are more photogenic than ever.

*Tourist office:*
*Rue du Pont-Levis,*
*4521Oudon*
*Tel: 02 40 83 80 04*

## Champtoceaux opposite

The town is worth a visit. You will have to climb a good kilometre to reach the summit of the rocky outcrop on which Champtoceaux has been built. At the top, you will be able to enjoy a 70 metre high view over the Loire and the keep on the opposite bank in Oudon. Leave your bicycle in the village square to follow the few hundred metres long Promenade de Champalud, an attractive "walkway" which leads past the ruins of the old fortress. If you do not go back down to the river, continue at least as far as the top of the Coulée de la Luce.

*Tourist office: Le Champalud,*
*49270 Champtoceaux,*
*Tel: 02 40 83 57 49*

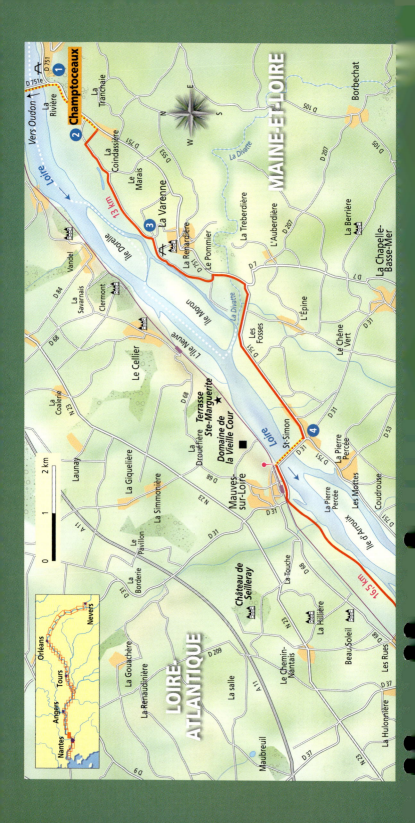

*Stage 17* / From Oudon-Champtoceaux to Nantes

## From shore to shore

◆ Champtoceaux is the starting point for the day and even if you have decided to spend the night in Oudon, you will not be able to avoid a detour via the village on the opposite shore!

Along the way, you will be able to deplore the fact that a bridge as recent as the one between Oudon and Champtoceaux has not been equipped with a simple cycle path. The traffic will prevent you from lingering there despite the fact that the view over the river is spectacular at all times of the year.

◆ On the left of the exit from the bridge, on the road up to Champtoceaux, do not miss the new picnic stopover which, situated opposite the river, below the terrace of a well-named restaurant-brasserie ("Le Port du Moulin"), allows you to admire the ruins of an old 13th-15th century mill. It also allows you to enjoy a river cruise on this section of the Loire aboard La Luce, an open-top tourist barge, which, from April to October, offers many interesting excursions along this stretch of the river (Tel: 02 40 83 57 49).

**❶ At the foot of Champtoceaux,** the route starts with a good climb, unfortunately shared with the traffic on the **D 751**. However, it is unavoidable with the planned path along the riverside not yet being operational.

**❷** Fortunately, after about a kilometre, the small road which leads off to the right towards **La Bridonnière** is the complete opposite. Running along a covered stretch of comfortable asphalt, this section is as peaceful as it is refreshing. The Loire (more precisely the "boire d'Anjou") is very near, even if you are barely able to see it until you reach **La Varenne** (campsite and picnic area where quiet is guaranteed) and there is hardly any traffic.

**❸** The crossing of the small valley just after **La Varenne** means having to return to the **D 751** again and you will continue along it until **Saint-Simon** and the Pont des Mauves.

◆ You will then find yourself on **La Divatte**, a long Loire levee covering several kilometres which, in the same way as the others, is designed to contain the river's potential excesses.

**❹** Cross the huge metal bridge to rejoin the right bank in **Mauves** and the almost continuous stretch of cyclist-only path to **Nantes** barely twenty kilometres further on.

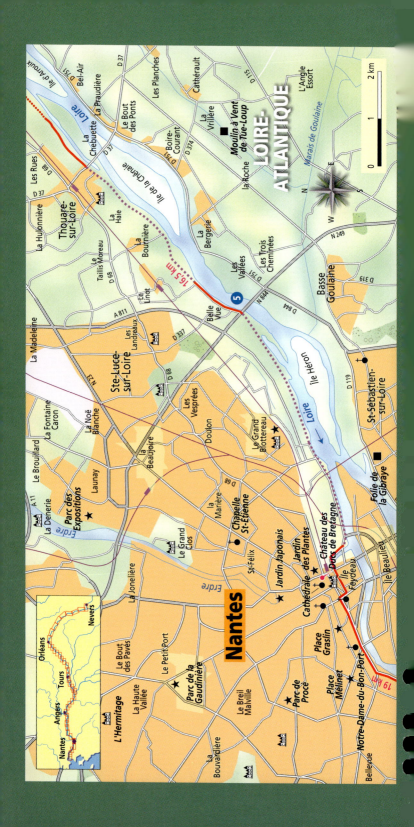

## Stage 17 / From Oudon-Champtoceaux to Nantes

◆ The end of the stage is almost completely straight. A proper cycle path followed by a series of small roads or hiking paths lead to **Thouaré-sur-Loire**, **La Bournière** and **Bellevue**.

5 After passing over the Nantes-Basse-Goulaine dual-carriageway, the very irregular path gradually enters the city of Nantes before arriving on the **quaysides of the Loire** along a cycle path leading to **Marcel-Saupin stadium**. Be careful, the cycle paths now run through the very dense traffic….

If necessary, the silhouette of the **castle of the Dukes of Brittany** all shiny and new, after 15 years of restoration work (photo above) is there to show you the way to the city centre.

*On La Divatte levee.*

## Stage 18
# From Nantes to Saint-Brévin-l'Océan 56 km

⬥ One of the route's great surprises, the crossing of the estuary by ferry (free) between Couëron/Port-Launay and Le Pellerin (opposite), the discovery trail along the astonishing Canal de la Martinière (about twenty kilometres), and, before arriving at the Atlantic coast in Saint-Brévin, the final stretch along the embankment to the foot of the bridge in Saint-Nazaire.

*Stage 18* / From Nantes to Saint-Brévin-l'Océan

## Nantes in brief

Young, dynamic, conquering, the "capital" of Loire-Atlantique, along with its neighbour Angers, is yet another French city where life is good. Although the proactive public transport policy has only partially freed it from the grip of motorised traffic, the cycle paths and car-free roads do allow you to explore the centre without difficulty. From Lieu Unique (the former Lu biscuit factory, now a cultural centre, Tel: 02 40 12 14 34) to Place Graslin via Passage Pommeraye and the pedestrianised streets of the old town centre, it is possible to ride almost anywhere without the stress of traffic. You can visit Saint-Pierre-Saint-Paul cathedral and continue north to the basin and shores of the River Erdre, which, within the space of a few years, has become a popular neighbourhood which bears a passing resemblance to Amsterdam.

The star of the show, the city's jewel is none other than the Castle of the Dukes of Brittany! Reopened to visitors in spring 2007, this stunning building, which has just undergone fifteen years of renovation work, has been a major event in the city. The feudal enclosure (restored walls and moats) shelters a sumptuous Renaissance-style ducal residence, which, restored and redesigned for visitors, now offers one of the most modern and educational History museums in France.

### Castle of the Dukes of Brittany,
Tel: 02 51 17 49 99,
www.château-nantes.fr

*Also in Nantes, do not miss*
→ The Museum of Fine Arts, 10, rue Georges-Clemenceau (behind Saint-Pierre-Saint-Paul Cathedral), one of the richest in France with a range of pictorial works from the 13th century to the 20th century, including works by Sisley and Kandinsky.
Tel: 02 51 17 45 00
→ La Cigale. On Place Graslin, a brasserie with a flamboyant ceramic decor.
Tel: 02 51 84 94 94
→ The Jules-Verne Museum, 3, rue de l'Hermitage. Born in Nantes, the author of Twenty Thousand Leagues under the Sea is well worth a visit.
Tel: 02 40 69 72 52
→ The "Estuary" event. For its final edition, programmed throughout summer 2011, this artistic route aims to open up Nantes to its estuary and to offer the opportunity to discover some exceptional sites.
→ River cruises.
On the Erdre and the Loire, an opportunity to discover the real river during an outing, a lunch or a dinner.
Bateaux Nantais, quai Motte Rouge
Tel: 02 40 14 51 14

**Tourist office
Greater Nantes:
2, place Saint-Pierre,
44000 Nantes
Tel: 0892 464 044**

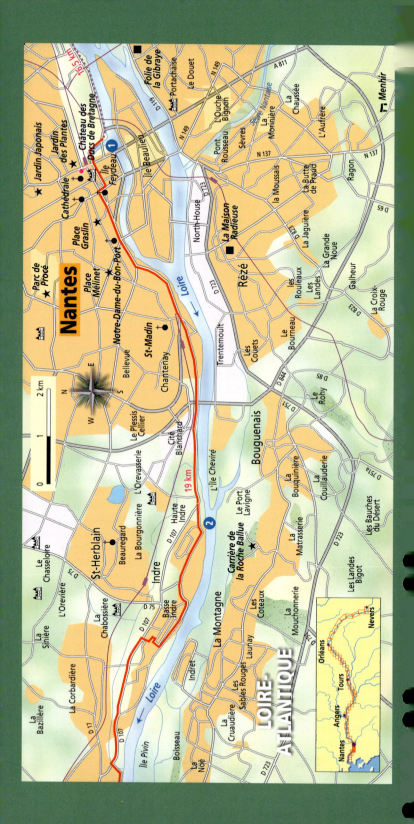

## Stage 18 / From Nantes to Saint-Brévin-l'Océan

### In the Pays d'Audubon

It was here in Couëron and the surrounding marshes that the naturalist Jean-Jacques Audubon (1785-1851) spent his childhood, developing such a passion for the many waterside birds that he decided to devote his life to them. He started by drawing them, then, after emigrating to the United States, by painting them, with an attention to observation and detail which made him one of the pioneers of the world of ecology. Most French people are not aware that with 500,000 members, the National Audubon Society is now the largest nature protection association!

### Towards the estuary

❶ Towards the sea and the estuary, the *Loire à vélo* trail leaves Nantes along the cycle routes and shared routes which offer a relative feeling of priority, or at least of safety.

◆ It is no surprise that, after the **Quai de la Fosse**, you quickly arrive in a port area with a high-level of industrial and commercial activity.

◆ The route – more often than not shared with the **D 107** – only starts to become more attractive when it leaves the built-up area.

*An air of Amsterdam in Nantes: Quai H. Barbusse on the River Erdre.*

❷ Once it arrives in **Haute-Indre**, and even more so in **Basse-Indre**, the landscape finally starts to become more natural.

145

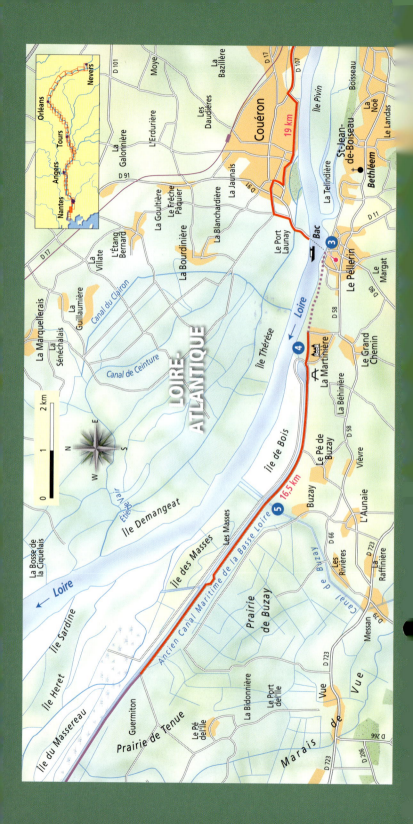

## Stage 18 / From Nantes to Saint-Brévin-l'Océan

*The greenway of the Canal of La Martinière.*

**3** In **Port-Launay**, just after **Couëron**, take the second ferry across the estuary which provides a regular and frequent (every 20 minutes) transfer from one shore to the other, with a two or three minute journey to the small town of **Pellerin** and its attractively redesigned quaysides.

After **Pellerin**, the cycle route, clearly signposted, leads directly to **La Martinière** along the riverside. A wonderful surprise awaits you in the form of one of the most interesting sites on the Nantes-Saint-Brévin section, and, above all one of the most natural: the old maritime canal of Basse-Loire, now a haven of peace.

**4** At the **Lock of La Martinière**, two parallel asphalt roads (the one on the left bank is ideal for rollerbladers) run along both banks of the wide canal. Opt for the one on the left bank which offers more shade if it is sunny and is better suited to picnic stops!

**5** 3 km further on, the canal crosses another lock, which allows the two paths to join each other and the canal becomes more open and more airy than on the first part. The remaining 4 km – take the route on the left – offer an outstanding journey along **Massereau Island**, the ornithological reserve on the opposite bank, where heron, duck, grebe, swan and others will not escape the eyes and ears of (silent) bicycle eco-tourists.

|147

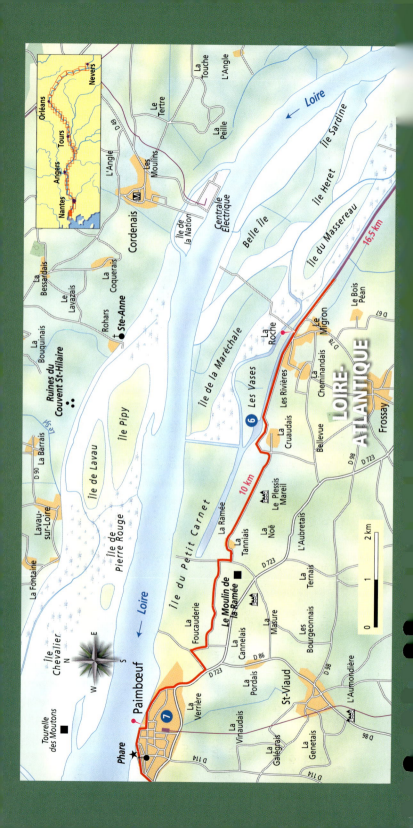

## Stage 18 / From Nantes to Saint-Brévin-l'Océan

**6** At **La Cruaudais**, the canal veers slightly to return back to the estuary: it was here that the ships travelling to Nantes entered the waterway specially dug for them.

◆ The cycle route **starts by heading south** before continuing **westwards** towards **Paimbœuf**, about half a dozen kilometres further on (via la Tagnais).

In any case, **it's difficult to go wrong** since the route was clearly and systematically signposted "Loire à Vélo" in 2009. Simply follow the signposts to stay on the right path!

**7** In any case, **Paimbœuf** is not far away and even if the view which the small town offers over the Loire is not the most natural in the sector (there are more attractive views than these over the Donges refineries!), it is here that the estuary is the most impressive. Between two worlds devoted to leisure (La Baule-Pornichet to the north, Saint-Brévin and its beaches to the south) the economic and industrial challenges of this sector are easy to understand. The movement of the cargo ships, the lights of the refineries and, in the distance, the long access ramps and the central span of Saint-Nazaire Bridge are not without reason.

*Sunset on Saint-Brévin beach.*

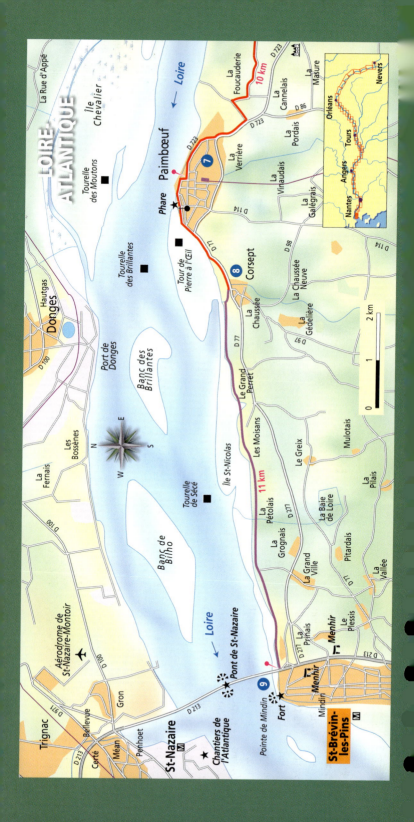

## Stage 18 / From Nantes to Saint-Brévin-l'Océan

◆ On **the D 77**, between **Paimbœuf** and Corsept, 3 km of shared road precede the very last section which offers the possibility of following a cyclist-only path along the south bank of the estuary. For this, follow the embankment (called Corsept) which runs for about ten kilometres along a narrow and rough path (mountain bikes recommended).

⑧ At **Corsept**, cyclists in a hurry may opt to continue to the end along the D 77.

◆ But a safer route does exist. The series of small roads leading via **La Mulotais**, **La Pitardais** and **La Prinais** to the bridge, which, less direct than the previous one, do offer a safe route to the end of the stage.

⑨ In all cases, **the centre of Saint-Brévin** is a short distance away. Ride there along **Avenue de Mindin**, and the coastal avenues separating the villas from the beach, as far as **the Plage des Pins** and **Le Pointeau**. Continue to **Saint-Brévin-l'Océan**, the most recent and liveliest part of the resort.

### Saint-Brévin in brief

The resort has been chosen as the end — and ocean — town of the *Loire à vélo* trail, and it took a while before this was recognised, in order for you to celebrate the event, or simply to allow you to lay claim to the honour.

This small resort also offers an attractive long beach, the discreet charm of which has, for many years (it was created in the 19th century), been the joy of those who have not fallen for the vanities of the opposite shore. You will just have to choose your beach: there are two here separated from each other by the Pointe du Pointeau: the beach of Saint-Brévin-les-Pins and of Saint-Brévin-l'Océan!

*Tourist office: 10, rue de l'Eglise, 44250 Saint-Brévin-les-Pins*
*Tel: 02 40 27 24 32*

◆ Along the river bank, you come to **the Pointe de Mindin**, passing beneath the ramp of Saint-Nazaire Bridge. You will arrive at Le **Débarcadère**, at the site from where the Saint-Nazaire ferries used to depart before the bridge was built. Finishing point of the *Loire à Vélo* trail.

## Excursion
# North estuary, south estuary

› There is a great temptation, once you have reached the "end of the road", to continue along the Atlantic coast to the north or the south of the estuary. However, there is a sizeable problem on the north side: Saint Nazaire Bridge is practically impassable by bicycles! This is a pity, because the Vélocéan route to the Guérande Peninsula and the Morbihan Department offers a large choice of cycle paths and reserved routes. However, to the south, the way is free to Pornic and Vendée.......

## A bridge too narrow!

Saint-Nazaire Bridge built at the start of the 1970s was quite simply designed solely for cars: the tiny pavement on both sides of the two roads are not designed for cyclists and it is highly inadvisable to ride along the road which is dangerously close to the traffic – unless very early in the morning or very late at night.

What should you do? Since the bus solution is not yet available (a coach link with Saint-Nazaire which carries bicycles), the hypothesis of a ferry (only during the tourist season) still being studied, the only way of crossing to the other side to Saint-Nazaire is to use a private car, or a taxi able to carry bicycles. The tourist office in Saint-Brévin may be able to help you.

This is all the more regrettable since the north coast of Loire-Atlantique has a particularly large choice of bicycle excursions. After Saint-Marc beach, the home of Jacques Tati, Pornichet, La Baule and Le Pouliguen, there are many wonderful opportunities to ride to Le Croisic or Piriac along the coast, as well as the Vélocéan route through the Guérande marshes.

To the south, things have become easier since Saint-Brévin completed its coastal route. The signposted Vélocéan route now leads to Pornic, with the following sections to the south of the department being provided by the generous Vendée cycle path network. Pornic is less than 20 km from the end of the *Loire à vélo* trail: the road to Bourgneuf (then to Noirmoutier, the Vendée and, even further, to Charente-Maritime) is now open to all cycling enthusiasts who prefer river cruises of the two-wheeled variety!

*Pornic, on the south road.*

> *Loire à vélo trail*
# Practical Information

## Bicycle hire "Accueil Vélo"

Listed in order of geographic location along the *Loire à vélo* trail, these bicycle hire/repair companies are committed to offering privileged equipment, service and a warm welcome to new bicycle tourists. Some of them ("Détours de Loire" in Tours, Blois and Saumur, and "Loire Vélo Nature" in Bréhémont among others) offer the advantage of multiple hire points.

**SANCERRE-SAINT-SATUR**
- Loire Nature Découverte,
quai de Loire, 18300 Saint-Satur,
Tel: 02 48 78 00 34 or 02 48 79 46 19
www.loirenaturedecouverte.com

**SAINT-JEAN-DE BRAYE**
- Loc. Val de Loire
117 avenue Charles-Péguy
45800 Saint-Jean de Braye
Tel: 02 38 84 11 78
www.loc-val-de-loire.com

**ORLEANS**
- Kit Loisirs, 7 avenue Dauphine,
45100 Orléans, Tel: 02 38 66 57 81
www.kitloisirs.com

**CHAMBORD**
- Traineurs de Loire, place Saint-Louis,
41250 Chambord, Tel: 02 54 33 37 54
www.traineursdeloire.com
- Other hire points in Blois and Cheverny.

**BLOIS**
- Rando Vélo, 2, rue Jean-Moulin,
and 29 rue du Puits-Neuf, 41000 Blois,
Tel: 02 54 78 62 52 or 06 89 56 26 48
www.randovelo.fr

**MOSNES**
**(between Chaumont and Amboise)**
- Fantasy Forest, 12 rue des Thomeaux,
37530 Mosnes, Tel: 02 47 30 50 90
www.domainedesthomeaux.fr

**AMBOISE**
- Locacycles, 2 bis rue Jean-Jacques-Rousseau, 37400 Amboise,
Tel: 02 47 57 00 28

**BLOIS, TOURS, SAUMUR and NANTES**
- Détours de Loire: 35 rue Charles-Gille,
37000 Tours, Tel: 02 47 61 22 23
www.locationdevelos.com
- Other hire points in Nevers, La Charité-sur-Loire, Sancerre, Briare, Sully-sur-Loire, Orléans, Beaugency, Blois, Cheverny, Amboise, Chenonceaux, Vouvray, Rochecorbon, Villandry, Langeais, Chinon, Les Rosiers-sur-Loire, Saumur, Angers, Montjean-sur-Loire, Ancenis, Nantes and Saint-Nazaire (with option of picking up the bicycle at one point and dropping it off at another).

**AZAY-LE-RIDEAU**
Cycles Leprovost
13 rue Carnot
37190 Azay-le-Rideau
Tel: 02 47 45 40 94

## *Loire à vélo trail* / Practical Information

**BREHEMONT**
• Loire Vélo Nature, 7 rue des Déportés, 37130 Bréhémont, Tel: 06 03 89 23 14
E-mail: celine@loirevelonature.com
• Other hire points in Blois, Chenonceaux, Tours, Villandry, Rillé, Chinon, Saumur and Angers.

**CHINON**
• Chinon Loisirs Activités Nature, quai Danton, 37500 Chinon, Tel: 06 23 82 96 33
www.loisirs-nature.fr

**LA DAGUENIERE (south of Angers)**
• Vélo Passion, place des Acacias, 49800 La Daguenière, Tel: 02 41 69 07 76
E-mail: velopassion2@wanadoo.fr

**LES PONTS-DE-CÉ**
• Cycles Cesbron, 2 avenue Gallieni, 49130 Les Ponts-de-Cé,
Tel: 02 41 44 87 44

**ANGERS**
Tourist Office: Angers Loire Tourisme, 7, place Kennedy, 49051 Angers Cedex 02,
Tel: 02 41 23 50 00
www.angersloiretourisme.com

**LA POMMERAYE**
**(between Chalonnes and Montjean)**
Michel Thomas/Campsite de la Guyonnière, 49620 La Pommeraye,
Tel: 02 41 77 78 05

## *Tour operators/Package holidays*

• Loire Valley Travel/Randovelo Travel
2, rue Jean-Moulin,
41000 Blois
Tel: 02 54 78 62 52
www.randovelo.fr

• Détours de Loire
35 rue Charles Gilles - 37000 Tours
Tel: 02 47 61 22 23

• Loire Vélo Nature
7 rue des Déportés - 37130 Bréhémont
Tel: 06 03 89 23 14

## Bicycle accommodation "Accueil Vélo"

A very large number of the hotels, gites, campsites and bed & breakfasts cited here have the "La Loire à Vélo" certification. This means that they have been the object of a certification guaranteeing a suitable standard of reception: a closed area for bicycles, an appropriate restaurant service, repair equipment and other services. Apart from a few exceptions, they are always near the main route and, as such, are recommended stopovers.

### Stage 1: From Nevers to La Charité

**NEVERS**
- Hotel Mercure Loire***,
quai de Médine, 58000 Nevers,
Tel: 03 86 93 93 86,
E-mail: H3480@accor.com
- Hotel Kyriad**, 35 boulevard Victor-Hugo, 58000 Nevers,
Tel: 03 86 71 95 95,
E-mail: kyriadnevers@wanadoo.fr
- Hotel-Restaurant Ibis**,
3 rue du Plateau-de-Bonne-Dame,
58000 Nevers, Tel: 03 86 37 56 00,
E-mail: H0947@accor.com

**CHALLUY**
- Bed & breakfast "Le Pavillon"
Stéphanie and Nicolas Goddet,
Tel: 03 86 90 30 39

**GIMOUILLE**
- Le Grand Bois, La Résidence****,
66 luxury wood cottages
Route de Fertôt, 58470 Gimouille,
Tel: 03 86 21 09 21

**MARSEILLES-LES-AUBIGNY**
- Bed & breakfast
chez Mr & Mrs de Champs, Château vert,
18320 Marseilles-les-Aubigny,
Tel: 02 48 76 04 91
www.chambredhote-chateauvert.com

### Stage 2: From La Charité to Sancerre

**LA CHARITÉ-SUR-LOIRE**
- Hotel Le Grand Monarque***,
33 quai Clemenceau, 58400
La Charité-sur-Loire, Tel: 03 86 70 21 73,
E-mail: le.grand.monarque@wanadoo.fr
- Hotel Le Bon Laboureur**,
quai Romain-Mollot,
58400 La Charité-sur-Loire,
Tel: 03 86 70 22 85,
E-mail: lebonlaboureur@wanadoo.fr
- Bed & breakfast
Christine Tardif, 9 rue du Pont,
58400 La Charité-sur-Loire,
Tel: 03 86 70 11 25,
E-mail: logisdupont@wanadoo.fr
- Bed & breakfast, Château de Gérigny
Delphine and Yann Lepessec-Polge,
Tel: 09 71 41 12 05,
E-mail: chateau-de-gerigny@wanadoo.fr

**HERRY**
- Bed & breakfast chez Mr Driessen,
le Lac, 18140 Herry,
Tel: 02 48 79 45 99
www.maisonlelac.com

**POUILLY-SUR-LOIRE**
- Hotel Le Relais de Pouilly***,
quai de Loire, 58150 Pouilly-sur-Loire,
Tel: 03 86 39 03 00
info@relaisdepouilly.com
- Hotel Le Coq Hardi**,
42 avenue de la Tuilerie,
58150 Pouilly-sur-Loire,
Tel: 03 86 39 12 99,
E-mail: lecoqhardi@orange.fr
- Bed & breakfast La Pouillyzote
Anne-Marie Rommel,
58150 Pouilly-sur-Loire, Tel: 03 86 39 17 98
- Bed & breakfast
Mr & Mrs Chamoux-Martinet,
place de la République,
58150 Pouilly-sur-Loire,
Tel: 03 86 39 15 58

**SANCERRE**
- Hotel Le Clos Saint-Martin***,
10 rue Saint-Martin, 18300 Sancerre,
Tel: 02 48 54 21 11

### Stage 3: From Sancerre to Briare

**SAINT-SATUR**
- Hotel de la Loire***,
2 quai de Loire, 18300-Saint-Thibault,
Tel: 02 48 78 22 22
www.hotel_de_la_loire.com

## Loire à vélo trail / Practical Information

**BANNAY**
- Hotel-Restaurant La Buissonnière,
58 rue du Canal, 18300 Bannay,
Tel: 02 48 72 42 07
www.labuissonniere.fr

**BOULLERET**
- Auberge de la Poularde**,
6 place de l'Eglise, 18240 Boulleret,
Tel: 02 48 72 32 56
www.aubergedelapoularde.com

**COSNE-COURS-SUR-LOIRE**
- Bed & breakfast Prieuré Saint-Agnan
Christine Grillères, place Saint-Agnan,
58200 Cosne-sur-Loire,
Tel: 06 99 03 07 75
- Bed & breakfast L'Orée des Vignes
Marie-Noëlle Kandin, 58200 Saint-Père,
Tel: 03 86 28 12 50

**CHATILLON-SUR-LOIRE**
- Campsite municipal "Les Combles",
route de Bourges, 45360 Chatillon-
sur-Loire, Tel: 02 38 31 42 92

**BRIARE**
- Hotel du Cerf**, 22 boulevard Buyser,
45250 Briare, Tel: 02 38 37 00 30
www.hotelducerfcom
- Auberge du Pont-Canal**,
19 rue du Pont-Canal, 45250 Briare,
Tel: 02 38 31 24 24

### Stage 4:
### From Briare to Sully-sur-Loire

**GIEN**
- Hotel Le Sanotel**, 21 quai de Sully,
45500 Gien, Tel: 02 86 67 61 46
www.sanotel.fr
- Campsite "Les Bois du Bardelet",
rue des Iris, Poilly-lez-Gien,
Tel: 02 38 67 47 39
- Campsite Touristique de Gien,
route d'Orléans, Poilly-lez-Gien,
Tel: 02 38 67 12 50

**SAINT-AIGNAN-LE-JAILLARD**
- Bed & breakfast La Ferme de l'Epinoy,
lieu-dit l'Epinoy, 45600 Saint-Aignan-
le-Jaillard, Tel: 02 36 36 29 73

**SULLY-SUR-LOIRE**
- Hotellerie du Château**, 4 route
de Paris, 45600 Saint-Père-sur-Loire,
Tel: 02 38 36 62 40
- Bed & breakfast "La Ferme des
Gorgeats", chemin de la Levée,
45600 Sully-sur-Loire,
Tel: 02 38 36 62 60
- Campsite Hortus "Le Jardin de Sully",
D 60, La Bergevinerie, 45600 Sully-Saint-
Père-sur-Loire, Tel: 02 38 36 35 94

### Stage 5:
### From Sully-sur-Loire to Orléans

**SANDILLON**
- Hotel "Un Toit Pour Toi"**,
2 rue de la Villette, 45640 Sandillon,
Tel: 02 38 41 00 22

**SAINT-JEAN-DE-BRAYE**
- Hotel Promotel**,
117 rue du Faubourg-de-Bourgogne,
45800 Saint-Jean-de-Braye,
Tel: 02 38 53 64 09
- Hotel Novotel Orléans/Saint-Jean-
de-Braye***, 145 avenue de Verdun,
Tel: 02 38 84 65 65

**ORLEANS**
- Hotel Escale Oceania**,
16 quai Saint-Laurent, 45000 Orléans,
Tel: 02 38 54 47 65
- Hotel de l'Abeille **,
64 rue Alsace-Lorraine (200 m from
the railway station), Tel: 02 38 53 54 87
- Grand Hotel**, 1 rue de la Lionne,
45000 Orléans, Tel: 02 38 53 19 79

### Stage 6:
### From Orléans to Beaugency

**LA CHAPELLE-SAINT-MESMIN.**
- Hotel Orléans Parc Hotel***,
55 route d'Orléans,
45380 La Chapelle-Saint-Mesmin,
Tel: 02 38 43 26 26
- Hotel-Restaurant "L'Escale du Port
Arthur"**, à Saint-Hilaire-Saint-Mesmin,
Tel: 02 38 76 30 36.

**TAVERS**
- Hotel la Tonnellerie****,
12 rue des Eaux-Bleues, 45190 Tavers,
Tel: 02 38 44 68 15

**BEAUGENCY**
- Hotel de la Sologne **,
6 place Saint-Firmin, 45190 Beaugency,
Tel: 02 38 44 50 27
www.hoteldelasologne.com
- Hotel "Le Relais des Templiers"**,
68 rue du Pont, 45190 Beaugency,
Tel: 02 38 44 53 78 –
www.hotelrelaistempliers.com
- Grand Hotel de l'Abbaye**,
2 quai de l'Abbaye, 45190 Beaugency,
Tel: 02 48 35 10 10

**Stage 7: From Beaugency to Blois**

**COURBOUZON**
- Bed & breakfast "Le Presbytère",
13 rue de Champsort,
41500 Courbouzon, Tel: 02 54 81 23 10

**MUIDES-SUR-LOIRE**
- Campsite municipal "Belle Vue"**,
Tel: 02 54 87 01 56
http://perso.wanadoo.fr/mairie-muides
- Campsite "Le Château des Marais"****,
27 rue de Chambord,
Tel: 02 54 87 05 42
www.château-des-marais. com

**SAINT-DYE-SUR-LOIRE**
- Hotel "Le Manoir de Bel-Air"***,
1 route d'Orléans, 41500 Saint-Dyé-
sur-Loire, Tel: 02 54 81 60 10
www.manoirbelair.com

**LA FERTE-SAINT-CYR**
- Hotel "Saint-Cyr", 15 faubourg
de Bretagne, 41220 La Ferté-Saint-Cyr,
Tel: 02 54 87 90 51
www.hotel-st-cyr.com

**CROUY-SUR-COSSON**
- Rural gites "Le moulin de Crouy"
(3 ears of corn), Nathalie Harrault,
3 Route de la Cordellerie, 41220
Crouy-sur-Cosson, Tel: 02 54 87 56 19
www.lemoulindecrouy.com

**THOURY**
- Bed & breakfast "La Ferme
de la Maugerie" (3 ears of corn),
8 route de la Maugerie, Tel: 02 54 87 05 07
www.la-maugerie.com

**BRACIEUX**
- Hotel de la Bonheure **,
9 bis rue René-Masson, 41250 Bracieux,
Tel: 02 54 46 41 57
- Hotel du Cygne **,
20 rue Roger-Brun, Tel: 02 54 46 41 07
www.hotelducygne.com
- Hotel L'Orée des Châteaux**,
9 bis route de Blois, 41250 Bracieux,
Tel: 02 54 46 47 14
- Campsite des Châteaux ***,
11 rue Roger-Brun, Tel: 02 54 46 41 84
www.campingdeschateaux.com

**VINEUIL**
- Hotel-Restaurant Campanile**,
48 rue des 4-Vents, 41350 Vineuil,
Tel: 02 54 42 70 22
www.campanile.fr
- Bed & breakfast "Le Clos Fleuri",
D 33, 41350 Vineuil, Tel: 02 54 42 74 90

**LA CHAUSSEE-SAINT-VICTOR**
- Hotel Tourhotel - La Chaussée-
Saint-Victor**, 23 route d'Orléans,
RN 152, 41260 La Chaussée-Saint-Victor,
Tel: 02 54 78 48 98
www.hoteltourhotel.com

**SAINT-DENIS-SUR-LOIRE**
- Hotel-Restaurant "Le Grand
Atelier"****, rue du 8-Mai-1945,
41000 Saint-Denis-sur-Loire,
Tel: 02 54 74 10 64
- Bed & breakfast "Harmonies",
Villeneuve, 41000 Saint-Denis-sur-Loire,
Tel: 02 54 74 16 45

**HUISSEAU-SUR-COSSON**
- Bed & breakfast "Château de
Nanteuil", 41350 Huisseau-sur-Cosson,
Tel: 02 54 42 61 98

**SAINT-GERVAIS-LA-FORÊT**
- Hotel-Restaurant Kyriad Blois sud,
320 rue de la Fédération,
41350 Saint-Gervais-la-Forêt,
Tel: 02 54 42 77 22

**Stage 8: From Blois to Amboise**

**BLOIS**
- Hotel "Anne de Bretagne"**,
31 avenue du Docteur-Jean-Laigret,
41000 Blois, Tel: 02 54 78 05 38
www.annedebretagne.free.fr
- Hotel-Restaurant "Le Monarque"**,
61 rue Porte-Chartraine, 41000 Blois,
Tel: 02 54 78 02 35
www.annedebretagne.free.fr
- Hotel-Restaurant "La Renaissance"**,
1 rue de la Garenne, 41000 Blois,
Tel: 02 54 78 02 63
www.hotel-renaissance.com
- Hotel "Côté Loire-Auberge
Ligérienne"***, 2 place de la Grève,
41000 Blois, Tel: 02 54 78 07 86
www.coteloire.com
- Hotel du Bellay*, 12 rue des Minimes,
41000 Blois, Tel: 02 54 78 23 62
- Centre Régional Jeunesse et Sports,
rue de la Taille-aux-Moines, 41000 Blois,
Tel: 02 54 52 20 40

**CANDE-SUR-BEUVRON**
- Hotel-Restaurant "La Caillère"***,
36, rue des Montils, 41120 Candé-
sur-Beuvron, Tel: 02 54 44 03 08

**CHAUMONT/ONZAIN**
- Bed & breakfast "La Maison
du Pêcheur", 123 rue du Maréchal-
de-Lattre-de-Tassigny, 41150 Chaumont-
sur-Loire, Tel: 02 54 20 91 47

- Campsite de Dugny, route de Chambon-sur-Cisse, 41150 Onzain, Tel: 02 54 20 70 66

### AMBOISE
- Hotel-Restaurant "Ibis Amboise"**, boulevard Saint-Denis, La Boitardière/Chargé (2 km upstream from Amboise), Tel: 02 47 23 10 23
- Hotel-restaurant Novotel Amboise***, 17 rue des Sablonnnières, 37400 Amboise, Tel: 02 47 57 42 07 E-mail: novotel.amboise@wanadoo.fr
- Hotel-restaurant "Le Vinci/Loire Valley"****, 12 avenue Emile-Gourin, 34400 Amboise, Tel: 02 47 57 10 90 www.vinciloirevalley.com

## Stage 9: From Amboise to Tours

### NAZELLES-NEGRON
- Hotel du Petit Lussault**, RD 959, route de Tours, 37530 Nazelles-Negron, Tel: 02 47 57 30 30

### AZAY-SUR-CHER
- Bed & breakfast "Le Clos des Augers" and organic eco-gite "Hameau des Augers", 37270 Les Augers, Tel: 02 47 50 49 49 www.auhameaudesaugers.fr

### VOUVRAY
- Bed & breakfast "Au Clos de l'Epinay", 37210 Vouvray, Tel: 02 47 52 61 90

## Stage 10: From Tours to Langeais

### TOURS
- Hotel de l'Univers****, 5 boulevard Heurteloup, 37000 Tours, Tel: 02 47 05 37 12 www.hotel-univers.fr
- Hotel Quality Harmonie***, 13 rue Frédéric-Joliot-Curie, 37000 Tours, Tel: 02 47 66 01 48 www.choicehotelseurope.com
- Hotel Moderne**, 1 and 3 rue Victor-Laloux, 37000 Tours, Tel: 02 47 05 32 81 – www.hotelmoderne37.com
- Hotel du Cygne - Contact Hotel **, 6 rue du Cygne, 37000 Tours, Tel: 02 47 66 66 41 www.hotel-cygne-tours.com
- Hotel de l'Europe **, 12 place du Maréchal-Leclerc, 37000 Tours, Tel: 02 47 05 42 07 E-mail: hotel-europe-tours@wanadoo.fr
- Hotel Kyriad Tours Centre***, 65 avenue de Grammont, 37000 Tours, Tel: 02 47 64 71 78 www.kyriad-tours-cbetween.fr
- Hotel Turone***, 4 place de la Liberté, 37000 Tours, Tel: 02 47 05 50 05 www.hotelturone.fr

### JOUÉ-LES-TOURS
- Hotel Escurial***, 4 et 8 rue EdouardBranly, 37300 Joué-les-Tours. Tel: 02 47 53 60 00 www.hotelescurial.com
- Hotel Mercure Tours-sud***, Parc des Bretonnières, 37300 Joué-les-Tours, Tel: 02 47 53 16 16 www.mercure.com
- Hotel "Ariane"**, 8 avenue du Lac, 37300 Joué-les-Tours, Tel: 02 47 67 67 60 www.hotel.ariane.com

### BALLAN-MIRÉ
- Campsite Airotel "La Mignardière"****, 22 avenue des Aubépines, 37510 Ballan-Miré. Tel: 02 47 73 31 00 www.mignardiere.com
- Bed & breakfast "Le Chateau des Templiers", 17 rue de la Commanderie, 37510 Ballan-Miré, Tel: 02 47 53 94 56

### SAVONNIÈRES
- Bed & breakfast "La Varinière" (2 ears of corn), M.C. Lisbona, 7 route des Grottes Pétrifiantes, 37510 Savonnières, Tel: 02 47 50 14 04 E-mail: lavariniere@yahoo.com

### VILLANDRY
- Hotel-Restaurant "Le Cheval Rouge" **, 9 rue Principale, 37510 Villandry, Tel: 02 47 50 02 07 E-mail: chevalrouge@creaweb.fr

## Stage 11: From Langeais to Chinon

### LANGEAIS
- Bed & breakfast "Anne de Bretagne" (3 ears of corn), 27 rue Anne-de-Bretagne, 37130 Langeais, Tel: 02 47 96 08 52

### BREHEMONT
- Villa-Cottage "Les Terrasses de Bréhémont" (3 keys), 37130 Bréhémont, Tel: 02 47 58 64 48 www.villacottage.com
- Bed & breakfast "L'Ancien Presbytère", 16 avenue du 11-Novembre, 37130 Bréhémont

**RIGNY-USSÉ**
- Bed & breakfast "La Petite Prée"
(3 ears of corn), 2 and 4 impasse
de la Petite-Prée, 37420 Rigny-Ussé,
Tel: 02 47 95 54 71

**SAINT-MICHEL-SUR-LOIRE**
- Auberge de la Bonde**
3, La Bonde, 37130 Saint-Michel-sur-Loire,
Tel: 02 47 96 83 13
E-mail: aubergedelabonde@wanadoo.fr

**SAVIGNY-EN-VERON**
- Campsite "La Fritillaire"***,
rue Basse, 37420 Savigny-en-Véron,
Tel: 02 47 58 03 79
www.cc-veron.fr/camping

**CHINON**
- Hotel "Agnès Sorel"**,
4 quai Pasteur, 37500 Chinon,
Tel: 02 47 93 04 37
www.agnes-sorel.com
- Hotel Le Chinon***, rue de la Digue-
Saint-Jacques, 37500 Chinon,
Tel: 02 47 98 04 37
www.lechinon.com

### Stage 12: From Chinon to Saumur

**MONTSOREAU**
- Hotel "Le Bussy"***,
4 rue Jeanne-d'Arc, 49730, Montsoreau,
Tel: 02 41 38 11 11
www.hotel-lebussy.fr
- Hotel La Marine de Loire***,
9 quai de la Loire, 49730 Montsoreau,
Tel: 02 41 50 18 21
www.hotel-lamarinedeloire.com
- Campsite de l'"Isle verte"***
49700 Montsoreau, Tel: 02 41 51 76 60
www.campingisleverte.com

**FONTEVRAUD-L'ABBAYE**
- Hotellerie La Croix Blanche**,
7 place des Plantagenêts,
49530 Fontevraud, Tel: 02 41 51 71 11
www.fontevraud.net

**TURQUANT**
- Hotel "Demeure de la Vignole"***,
3 impasse Marguerite-d'Anjou,
49730 Turquant, Tel: 02 41 53 67 00
www.demeure-vignole.com
- Bed & breakfast "La Turcane"
(3 ears of corn). Paula Tranchant,
4 ruelle de la Cour-du-Puits,
49730 Turquant, Tel: 02 41 38 37 44
www.la-turcane.fr
- Bed & breakfast "Le Balcon Bleu",
2 rue des Martyrs, 49730 Turquant,
Tel: 02 41 38 10 31

### Stage 13: From Saumur to Gennes

**SAUMUR**
- Hotel Mercure Bords de Loire***,
rue du Vieux-Pont, 49400 Saumur,
Tel: 02 41 67 22 42 - www.loire-hotel.fr
- Hotel Best Western "Adagio"***,
94 avenue du Général-de-Gaulle,
49400 Saumur, Tel: 02 41 67 45 30
www.hoteladagio.com
- Hotel du Parc**, 169 avenue
des Fusillés, 49400 Saumur,
Tel: 02 41 67 17 18
www.hotelduparc.fr
- Hotel "Saint-Pierre"****,
8 rue Haute-Saint-Pierre, 49400 Saumur,
Tel: 02 41 50 33 00
www.saintpierresaumur.com
- Hotel Alcyon**, 2 bis rue de Rouen,
49400 Saumur, Tel: 02 41 67 51 25
- Hotel Kyriad**, 23 rue Daillé,
49400 Saumur, Tel: 02 41 51 05 78
www.central-kyriad.com
- Cristal Hotel**, 12 place de la
République, 49400 Saumur,
Tel: 02 41 51 09 54
www.cristal-hotel.fr
- Hotel-Bed & breakfast "Château
de Verrières"*****,
53 rue d'Alsace, 49400 Saumur
www.chateau-verrieres.com
- Hotel "de Londres"**,
48 rue d'Orléans, 49400 Saumur,
Tel: 02 41 51 23 98
www.lelondres.com
- Hotel Le Volney**, 1 rue Volney,
49400 Saumur, Tel: 02 41 51 25 41
www.levolney.com
- Hotel "Anne d'Anjou"****,
32 quai Mayaud, Tel: 02.41.67.30.30
www.hotel-anneanjou.com
- Hotel "Le Nouveau Terminus"**,
15 avenue David d'Angers,
49400 Saumur, Tel: 02 41 67 31 01
Website: www.nouveau-terminus.com
- Hotel "Les Terrasses de Saumur"**,
chemin de l'Alat, Saint-Hilaire/Saint-
Florent, 49400 Saumur,
Tel: 02 41 67 28 48
www.clos-des-benedictins.fr
- Hotel Le Canter*,
1 place de la Sénatorerie,
49400 Saint-Hilaire/Saint-Florent,
Tel: 02 42 50 37 88 - www.lecanter.fr
- Campsite "de Chantepie"*****,
Saint-Hilaire/Saint-Florent,
49400 Saumur, Tel: 02 41 67 95 34
www.campingchantepie.com
- Campsite de l'Ile d'Offard****,
rue de Verden, 49400 Saumur,
Tel: 02 41 40 30 00
www.cvtloisirs.com/offard

*Loire à vélo trail* / Practical Information

• Centre International de Séjour,
rue de Verden, 49400 Saumur,
Tel: 02.41.40.30.00
www.cvtloisirs.com

### CHENEHUTTE-LES-TUFFEAUX
• Hotel "Le Prieuré"****,
49350 Chénehutte-les-Tuffeaux,
Tel: 02 41 67 90 14
www.prieure.com

### CUNAULT
• Bed & breakfast "Les Bateliers",
28 rue de Beauregard, 49350 Cunault,
Tel: 02 41 67 94 49
• Bed & breakfast "Beauregard",
Fanny Tonnelier, 22 rue Beauregard,
49350 Chènehutte-Trèves-Cunault,
Tel: 02 41 67 92 93
• Bed & breakfast "La Chauminette",
2 rue Foulques-Nerra, 49350 Preban,
Tel: 02 41 67 92 54

### SAINT-MARTIN-DE-LA-PLACE
• Hotel "Domaine de la Blairie"**,
5 rue de la Mairie,
49160 Saint-Martin-de-la-Place,
Tel: 02 41 38 42 98
www.hotel-blairie.com

**Stage 14: From Gennes to Angers**

### GENNES
• Hotel "Aux Naulets d'Anjou"**,
18 rue Croix-de-Mission, 49350 Gennes,
Tel: 02 41 51 81 88
www.hotel-lesnauletsdanjou.com
• Bed & breakfast "Les Fiefs Vaslin",
13 rue des Fiefs-Vaslin, 49350 Gennes,
Tel: 02 41 51 93 59
• Bed & breakfast "Le domaine
de Joreau", la Croix de Joreau,
49350 Gennes, Tel: 02 41 38 02 58
• Campsite "Au Bord de Loire" **,
avenue des Cadets-de-Saumur,
49350 Gennes, Tel: 02 41 38 04 67
www.camping-auborddeloire.com

### LES ROSIERS-SUR-LOIRE
• Hotel "Au val de Loire" **, place de
l'Eglise, 49350 Les Rosiers-sur-Loire,
Tel: 02 41 51 80 30
www.au-val-de-loire.com
• Campsite "Val de Loire"****,
6 rue Sainte-Baudruche,
49350 Les Rosiers-sur-Loire,
Tel: 02 41 51 94 33
www.camping-valdeloire.com
• Bed & breakfast "Domaine de l'Oie
Rouge", Christiane Batel, 8 rue
Nationale, 49350 Les Rosiers-sur-Loire,
Tel: 02 41 53 65 65
www.domaine-oie-rouge.fr

### LE THOUREIL
• Bed & breakfast "Le Clos de l'Abbaye",
Saint-Maur, 49350, Le Thoureil,
Tel: 02 41 79 09 38
• Bed & breakfast "La Haute Cormerie",
2 rue de la Cormerie, 49350 Le Thoureil,
Tel: 02 41 47 14 87
www.la-haute-cormerie.com

### COUTURES
• Campsite "Parc de Montsabert"****,
Montsabert, 49320 Coutures,
Tel: 02 41 57 91 63
www.parcdemontsabert.com

### LA DAGUENIERE
• Bed & breakfast chez Mr & Mrs Piers,
65 rue Ligérienne, 49800 La Daguenière,
Tel: 02 41 69 87 94

### LES PONTS-DE-CÉ
• Campsite de l'Ile du Château***,
avenue de la Boire-Salée,
49130 Les Ponts-de-Cé,
Tel: 02 41 44 62 05
www.camping-ileduchateau.com
• Hotel Kyriad**, 62 avenue Gallieni,
49130 Les Ponts-de-Cé,
Tel: 02 41 44 92 44 – www.kyriad.fr

### SAINTE-GEMMES-SUR-LOIRE
• Bed & breakfast "Le Ponceau",
4 route du Hutreau,
49130 Sainte-Gemmes-sur-Loire,
Tel: 02 41 79 20 52
www.loire-aubance.com

### BRAIN-SUR-L'AUTHION
• Campsite du Pont Caroline***,
rue du Pont-Caroline,
49800 Brain-sur-l'Authion,
Tel: 02 41 80 42 18

### ANGERS
• Hotel de France***, 8 place de la Gare,
49100 Angers, Tel: 02 41 88 49 42
www. Hoteldefrance-angers.com
• Campsite du Lac de Maine****,
avenue du Lac-de-Maine, 49000 Angers.
Tel: 02 41 73 05 03
www.camping-angers.fr
• Ethic Stages Lac de Maine,
49 avenue du Lac-de-Maine,
49000 Angers, Tel: 02.41.22.32.10
www.lacdemaine.fr
• Hotel de l'Europe**, 3 rue
Châteaugontier, 49100 Angers,
Tel: 02 41 88 67 45
www.hoteldeleurope-angers.com
• Hotel Continental**,
14 rue Louis-de-Romain,
49100 Angers, Tel: 02 41 86 94 94
www.hotellecontinental.com

- Hotel de Champagne**,
34 avenue Denis-Papin,
49100 Angers, Tel: 02 41 25 78 78
www.hoteldechampagne.fr
- Hotel d'Iéna**, 27 rue Marceau,
49100 Angers, Tel: 02 41 87 52 40
www.hotel-iena.com

## Stage 15: From Angers to Montjean
### BOUCHEMAINE
- Hotel "L'Ancre de marine"*,
place Ruzebouc, 49080 Bouchemaine,
Tel: 02 41 77 14 46
www.la-terrasse-sur-loire.com

### BEHUARD
- Bed & breakfast chez Francis and
Jeanne Krembel, 6 rue du Merdreau,
île de Béhuard, 49170 Béhuard,
Tel: 02 41 73 10 77

### ROCHEFORT-SUR-LOIRE
- Hotel "Le Grand Hotel"**,
30 rue René-Gasnier, 49190 Rochefort-sur-Loire, Tel: 02 41 78 80 46
www.le.grand.hotel.net
- Campsite de Saint-Offange***,
route de Savennières,
49190 Rochefort-sur-Loire,
Tel: 02 41 78 82 11
www.camping-rochefort49.com

### SAVENNIERES
- Aire naturelle de Camping
"La Bradière", 49170 Savennières,
Tel: 02 41 39 51 88
- Bed & breakfast chez Sylvette and
Philippe Leclerc, Moulin de Beaupréau,
49170 Savennières, Tel: 02 41 72 24 47
www.chambresaumoulin-savennieres.fr
- Bed & breakfast Lorcival, chez Evelyne
Marchesi, 3 place du Mail,
49170 Savennières, Tel: 02 42 72 28 10
E-mail: evelyne-marchesi@wanadoo.fr

### LA POSSONNIERE
- Hotel "La Taverne du Prieuré",
1 place du Pilori, 49170 La Possonnière,
Tel: 02 41 72 20 44
- Bed & breakfast "La Rousselière",
chez Mr & Mrs de Beru,
49170 La Possonnière,
Tel: 02 41 39 13 21
www.anjou-et-loire.com/rousselière

### SAINT-GEORGES-SUR-LOIRE
- Bed & breakfast "La Tour Girault",
Les Chesnaies, 18 Port Girault,
49170 Saint-Georges-sur-Loire,
Tel: 02 41 37 16 83

### CHALONNES-SUR-LOIRE
- Bed & breakfast "Beausoleil",
chez Mrs Perrault-Meskens,
64 rue Saint-Maurille,
49270 Chalonnes-sur-Loire,
Tel: 02 41 77 95 67

### LA POMMERAYE
- Campsite "La Guyonnière"**,
La Guyonnière, 49620 La Pommeraye,
Tel: 02 41 77 89 56
- Hotel "Les jardins de l'Anjou"**,
49620 La Pommeraye,
Tel: 02 41 35 11 00
www.hotel-anjou.com
- Bed & breakfast "Les Préaux",
chez Blandine Humeau, Les Préaux,
49620 La Pommeraye,
Tel: 02 41 39 03 14

## Stage 16:
## From Montjean to Champtoceaux
### MONTJEAN
- Hotel-Restaurant "Auberge
de la Loire"***, 2 quai des Mariniers,
49570 Montjean-sur-Loire,
Tel: 02 41 39 80 20
www.aubergedelaloire.com
- Bed & breakfast "Le Fief des
Cordeliers", lieu-dit Bellevue,
49570 Montjean-sur-Loire,
Tel: 02 41 43 96 09
www.lefiefdescordeliers.com
- Bed & breakfast "Les Cèdres",
17 rue du Prieuré,
49570 Montjean-sur-Loire,
Tel: 02 41 39 39 25
www.les-cedres.net
- Campsite de la Promenade ***,
La Maison Neuve, quai des Mariniers,
49570 Montjean-sur-Loire,
Tel: 02 41 39 02 68
www.camping.montjean.net

### INGRANDES-SUR-LOIRE
- Bed & breakfast chez Thérèse Douge,
10 place de l'Eglise,
49123 Ingrandes-sur-Loire,
Tel: 02 41 39 21 83
- Bed & breakfast "L'Amour de la Loire",
5 rue de l'Eglise,
49123 Ingrandes-sur-Loire,
Tel: 02 41 31 84 42
- Hotel-Restaurant « Le Lion d'Or »**,
26 rue du Pont,
49123 Ingrandes-sur-Loire,
Tel: 02 41 39 20 08
www.leliondor49.fr

## *Loire à vélo trail* / Practical Information

### LE MESNIL-EN-VALLEE
• Hotel "Au Poisson d'Argent"**,
Le Port, 49410 Le Mesnil-en-Vallée,
Tel: 02 41 78 96 12
www.aupoissondargent.com
• Bed & breakfast "Loire-Charmillles",
chez Mrs Nadia Leinberger,
9 rue des Ecoles,
49410 Le Mesnil-en-Vallée,
Tel: 02 41 78 94 74
www.loire-charmilles.com

### SAINT-FLORENT-LE-VIEIL/VARADES
• Campsite de l'île Batailleuse,
49410 Saint-Florent-le-Vieil,
Tel: 02 40 83 45 01
• Bed & breakfast, chez Jean-Pierre
Saint-Machin, la Grande Menuère,
44370 Varades,
Tel: 02 40 96 78 52 or 06 62 02 03 16

### LE MARILLAIS
• Bed & breakfast chez Danielle Gabory,
52 impasse du Coteau,
49410 Le Marillais, Tel: 02 41 72 75 78

### ANCENIS
• Hotel de la Loire**, le Jarrier d'Ancenis,
route d'Angers, 44150 Saint-
Herblon/Ancenis, Tel: 02 40 96 00 03
• Campsite de l'île Mouchet ***,
la Davrays, 44150 Ancenis,
Tel: 02 40 83 08 43
www.camping-estivance.com
• Hotel "Akwaba" **,
boulevard Docteur-Moutel,
44150 Ancenis, Tel: 02 40 83 30 30
www.hotel-akwaba.com

### Stage 17:
### From Champtoceaux to Nantes

### CHAMPTOCEAUX
• Hotel-Restaurant "Le Champalud"**,
place du Chanoine-Bricard, 49270
Champtoceaux, Tel: 02 40 83 50 09
www.lechampalud.com

### SAINTE-LUCE-SUR-LOIRE
• Bed & breakfast "Manoir du Grand
Plessis", route de Plessis,
44980 Sainte-Luce-sur-Loire,
Tel: 02 40 25 61 43 or 06 86 60 69 29
• Campsite Belle Rivière, route des
Perrières, 44980 Sainte-Luce-sur-Loire,
Tel: 02 40 25 85 81

### Stage 18:
### From Nantes to Saint-Brévin-les-Pins

### NANTES
• Hotel-Restaurant Mercure
"Ile de Nantes"***,
15 boulevard Alexandre-Millerand,
44200 Nantes,
Tel: 02 40 95 95 95
www.accorhotels.com
• Hotel "L'Hotel"***,
6, rue Henri-IV, 44000 Nantes,
Tel: 02 40 29 30 31
www.nanteshotel.com
• Hotel Saint-Yves**,
154 rue du Général-Buat, 44000 Nantes,
Tel: 02 40 74 48 42
• Hotel Duquesne**, 12 allée Duquesne
(cours des 50-Otages), 44000 Nantes,
Tel: 02 40 47 57 24
• Campsite du Petit Port,
2 boulevard du Petit-Port,
44300 Nantes

### COUERON
• Hotel "Etap Hotel"**, route de Vannes,
La Barrière Noire, 44220 Couëron,
Tel: 08 92 68 32 73
www.etaphotel.com

### LE PELLERIN
• Hotel-Restaurant "La Belle Epoque",
11 quai Provost, 44460 Le Pellerin,
Tel: 02 40 04 68 14

### SAINT-VIAUD (near Paimbœuf)
• Gîte de la Lande, 44320 Saint-Viaud,
Tel: 02 40 39 15 44

### CORSEPT
• Bed & breakfast La Pousada,
in La Fossiais, 44560 Corsept,
Tel: 02 40 39 13 54 or 06 11 46 50 13

### SAINT-BREVIN-LES-PINS
• Hotel-Restaurant "du Béryl"***,
55 boulevard de l'Océan,
44250 Saint-Brévin-les-Pins,
Tel: 02 28 53 20 00
www.groupe-emeraude.com
• Hotel-Restaurant "Le Débarcadère"**,
place Bougainville,
44250 Saint-Brévin-les-Pins,
Tel: 02 40 27 20 53
• Hotel-Restaurant "Le Petit Trianon"**,
239 avenue de Mindin,
44250 Saint-Brévin-les-Pins,
Tel: 02 40 27 22 16

# The Castles by Bicycle

The "Pays des Châteaux à Vélo": 300 km of cycle routes, brochure-map available on request
Pays de Châteaux, mairie de Bracieux, 41250 Bracieux
Tel: 02 54 46 09 30 – E-mail: pays-des-chateaux@wanadoo.fr

## Tourist offices

**Blois tourist office*****
23, place du Château
BP 199 - 41006 Blois Cedex
Tel: 02 54 90 41 41
Website: www.loiredeschateaux.com

**Bracieux tourist office**
10, Les Jardins du Moulin
41250 Bracieux
Tel/fax: 02 54 46 09 15

**Candé-sur-Beuvron tourist office***
10, route de Blois
41120 Candé-sur-Beuvron
Tel/fax: 02 54 44 00 44

**Cellettes tourist office**
2, rue de la Rozelle
41120 Cellettes
Tel/fax: 02 54 70 30 46

**Chambord Accueil**
Place Saint-Louis
41250 Chambord
Tel/fax: 02 54 33 39 16

**Chaumont-sur-Loire tourist office***
24, rue du Maréchal-Leclerc
41150 Chaumont-sur-Loire
Tel: 02 54 20 91 73
Website: www.chaumontsurloire.info

**Cheverny tourist office****
12, rue du Chêne-des-Dames
41700 Cheverny
Tel: 02 54 79 95 63

**Les Montils tourist office***
15 bis, route Haye
41120 Les Montils
Tel/fax: 02 54 44 05 07

**Muides-sur-Loire tourist office**
Place de la Libération
41500 Muides-sur-Loire
Tel: 02 54 87 58 36

**Saint-Dyé-sur-Loire tourist office***
73, rue Nationale
41500 Saint-Dyé-sur-Loire
Tel/fax: 02 54 81 65 45
Website: www.saint-dye-sur-loire.com

**Saint-Laurent-Nouan tourist office***
36, route d'Orléans
41220 Saint-Laurent-Nouan
Tel/fax: 02 54 87 01 31
and 08 75 32 00 72

# www.loire-a-velo.fr
# everything for planning your holidays

All practical information
can be viewed and downloaded
at **www.loire-a-velo.fr**

> contact details for accommodation and bike hire and repair outlets
> packages
> news and not-to-be-missed events
> downloadable routes for planning your overnight stays
> ideas for visits and exploring the area
... and much more!

# Acknowledgements

To all the designers, producers and communicators of the *Loire à vélo* trail.

To Jacques Auxiette, President of the Pays de la Loire region, and to Daniel Dupuis, President of the Pays de la Loire Tourist Board, to François Bonneau and François Dumon, President and Vice-President of Centre region, to Alain Beignet, President of the Loire Valley Tourist Board, to Dominique Tremblay, Director, and Nathalie Malaurie, Communication Director of the "Mission Val de Loire".

As well as to Corinnne Amigouët, Philippe Anquetil, Emilie Arribas, Aude Aucher, Philippe Audoin, Arlette Avrillon, Raymond Bablée, Yvelyne Batard, Yves Bergot, Brigitte Bigot, Annie Blin, Tiphaine Blot, Laurent Boron, Olivier Bouchereau, Samuel Buchwalder, Frédérique Colin, Isabelle Coquelet, Olivier Daumas, Fabrice Degat, Christine Deiss, Marion Demonteil, Quitterie de Pontis-Thellier, Jennifer Desille, Marie-Christine Dubois, Philippe Dubuy, Fanny Dorne, Nathalie Ferrand, Sandrine Fouret, Marion Frémont, Anne Gaborit, Antoine Héry, Jean-Philippe Javello, Lydia Labalette, Thierry Lacombe, Marie-Christine Lassery, Francis Legros, Sylvie Loué, Christophe Marzais, Mathias Maugard, Anne-Laure Morit, Anne-Cécile Olivier, Florence Petit, Virginie Priou, Hélène Ramsamy, Marie Rocher, Lygie Rothon, Isabelle Scipion, Françoise Thévenot who, at the departmental councils, departmental and regional Tourist Boards, communities of communes or urban districts provided their kind and invaluable assistance in the preparation of this book.

And, finally, to Editions Ouest-France which were the first to believe in the opportunity offered by this bike guidebook.

## By the same author

Editor: Aurélya Guerréro, Gaëlle Guilmard - Editorial coordination: Caroline Brou
Translation: Dédicace
Graphic design and page layout: Studio Graphique des Éditions Ouest-France
Photoengraving: Micro Lynx (35)
Printed by: Navis Print, Paris (15ᵉ)
© 2010, Editions Ouest-France - Edilarge SA, Rennes
ISBN 978-2-7373-5001-6 - Legal deposit : february 2010 - Editor No.: 6106.01.02.02.10

Visit us at www.editionsouestfrance.fr